SOCIETY AND SOLITUDE

CAMBRIDGE
UNIVERSITY PRESS

University Printing House, Cambridge CB2 8BS, United Kingdom

Cambridge University Press is part of the University of Cambridge.

It furthers the University's mission by disseminating knowledge in the pursuit of
education, learning and research at the highest international levels of excellence.

www.cambridge.org
Information on this title: www.cambridge.org/9781107585911

First published 1922
First paperback edition 2015

A catalogue record for this publication is available from the British Library

ISBN 978-1-107-58591-1 Paperback

SOCIETY AND SOLITUDE

BY

E. T. CAMPAGNAC

Professor of Education in the University of Liverpool

CAMBRIDGE
AT THE UNIVERSITY PRESS
1922

TO

C. S. J.

PREFACE

MY thanks are due, and I desire to pay them to a few friends who have had the kindness to read these chapters in manuscript and have given me the benefit of their criticism and advice, and then have been patient enough to help me in preparing them for the press.

And thanks, again, to the Editor of *The Times Educational Supplement* for his generous permission to use (in Chapters VII and VIII) parts of articles on "The Organisation of Ideals" and on "The Specialist of the Future" which I wrote for him several years ago.

And thanks, not least, to the officials of the Cambridge University Press for their care and their courtesy, both inexhaustible.

E. T. CAMPAGNAC.

ABERCROMBY HOUSE,
LIVERPOOL.
March, 1922.

ἀλλ' ἐπιμεληθείη μὲν ⟨ἂν⟩ ἄριστα καθ' ἕν καὶ ἰατρὸς καὶ
γυμναστὴς καὶ πᾶς ἄλλος ὁ καθόλου εἰδώς, τί πᾶσιν ἢ τοῖς τοιοισδί
(τοῦ κοινοῦ γὰρ αἱ ἐπιστῆμαι λέγονταί τε καὶ εἰσίν)· οὐ μὴν ἀλλ'
ἑνός τινος οὐδὲν ἴσως κωλύει καλῶς ἐπιμεληθῆναι καὶ ἀνεπιστή-
μονα ὄντα, τεθεαμένον δ' ἀκριβῶς τὰ συμβαίνοντα ἐφ' ἑκάστῳ δι'
ἐμπειρίαν, καθάπερ καὶ ἰατροὶ ἔνιοι δοκοῦσιν ἑαυτῶν ἄριστοι εἶναι,
ἑτέρῳ οὐδὲν ἂν δυνάμενοι ἐπαρκέσαι. οὐδὲν δ' ἧττον ἴσως τῷ γε
βουλομένῳ τεχνικῷ γενέσθαι καὶ θεωρητικῷ ἐπὶ τὸ καθόλου
βαδιστέον εἶναι δόξειεν ἄν, κἀκεῖνο γνωριστέον ὡς ἐνδέχεται·
εἴρηται γὰρ ὅτι περὶ τοῦθ' αἱ ἐπιστῆμαι.

ARISTOTLE ; Ethics X. ix. 16, 17.

CONTENTS

CHAPTER I

THE ETERNAL SOCIETY

Society—the earliest already governed by an ideal (1). Progress of civilisation, tests of. Labour and repose (2–3). The individual and society: difficulties and advantages of elementary forms of society: relationships few and simple: significance of parts in and for the whole more easily perceived than in a later and more elaborate society. Loss of unity and causes of this; both in the individual and in society itself (3–7). Variety and confusion. The separation of interest from interest (8). The recovery of unity, and the remaking of society. The spirit of man (9–10).

CHAPTER II

EDUCATION—THE MAKING OF SOCIETY AND ITS MEMBERS

Education the process by which men discover themselves: other accounts of education (12). Education, scientific and humane: the value and the danger of this distinction (13, 14). Specialisation and specialists (15). Variety and concentration (16). A man and his neighbours (18). Education and instruction (19). Analogy between society and the individual (22). Self-realisation and escape from self (23). The busy man (24). Distracting duties; society, the temporal and the eternal.

CHAPTER III

AGENTS AND PROCESSES

The safeguarding of the young (28). Parents unable to give the care and the time needed (29). They therefore employ deputies —caretakers or teachers (29, 30). This delegation of parental work to other persons dictated not only by economic necessity. The

CONTENTS

CHAPTER IV

NATURE AND DISCIPLINE

CHAPTER V

CONVERSATION WITH THE WORLD

CHAPTER VI

LIFE AND LANGUAGE

CHAPTER VII

SUBJECTS OF DISCOURSE

CHAPTER VIII

SCIENCE AND SCIENCES

CHAPTER IX

WORK AND PLAY

CHAPTER X

ORIGINALITY AND CONVENTION

CHAPTER XI

OURSELVES AND OUR NEIGHBOURS

CHAPTER XII

UNITY AND DIFFERENCE

CHAPTER XIII

ARTISTS AND MEN

CHAPTER XIV

THE TEACHER'S ART

Artists and players—professional players and gentlemen (189–191). The respectable amateur, and the would-be Bohemian. The concentration of the artist upon his task (192). Self-consciousness and disease; delicacy and health. The great vocation (194). The teacher an artist: arraigned as a fanatic and a tyrant, and often tempted to be both. Escape from these dangers (195–196). The teacher a creator—in what sense. The condition on which he traffics with the world.

CHAPTER XV

IMPRISONMENT AND FREEDOM

The present demand for education prompted by the desire for conversation, for entrance into the human society (199–200). Society and the best society: an educated society (201). Excellence won by limitation; resentment against limitation (203–206). Leisure and learning—and wisdom (208). Leisure and vacuity (212). Isolation and a common humanity (213).

CHAPTER XVI

SILENCE, MEDITATION AND PAIN

Emancipation (214). The language of parables (215). Destiny and vocation: vocation surpassed (216–217). Governor and governed (218–221). The fruits of education (222). Goodness uses knowledge and skill as instruments; but makes them more than instruments by absorbing them in itself (224). Listening to silence; the practice of meditation (225). Pain, suffered willingly and intelligently, hastens the coming of a new and unified society (226).

THE ETERNAL SOCIETY

I F by the slow steps of plodding research or by the quick passage of poetic imagination, we make our way back to the earliest time of which we have any records, or to the simplest forms of human existence which we can picture to ourselves, we find that already men lived in a society composed of different elements, each one of which justified its existence by contributing what it was best able to contribute and drawing from the others what they could provide more richly and abundantly in order to make good its own defects. But these services rendered and received, however various they were, had a common end, and that end was the maintenance of human life; and it is quite clear, whether we have recourse to the evidence of historians or to the more penetrating and subtle evidence of poets, that man's life did not consist even in its barest, rudest form in the things which he ate, the garments with which he was clothed, or of any or all of the material things without which, it is true, his life could not have been maintained. The labours, super-human as we sometimes call them, which primitive people endured in order to live, they endured not merely in order to live, but in order to live in a certain way which seemed to them good. To be men, they must be more than men: the work which they did was directed towards an ideal, and it was this ideal which co-ordinated and gave unity to the various special kinds of work into which their general and common labours were already divided.

The progress of civilisation is marked and tested by two criteria; first, we may say that it is a natural and proper ambition for men to achieve the things which are necessary to the maintenance of life so effectually and so speedily as that they may have an ever increasing security and an ampler leisure for the enjoyment of their ideal, whatever it may be; but, and this is the second criterion, we may with equal truth affirm that the progress of civilisation is marked by the vividness and reality with which men can apprehend (not only when their labours are done, but in the very process of those labours) the ideal itself for the sake of which they were undertaken. For a man cannot be content unless he is able both to delight *in* his work and to rest *from* his labour. But these conditions of happiness depend upon other conditions, or, rather, they need to be more fully stated. If, then, a man is to delight in his work, he must be convinced that the particular occupation in which he is at any moment engaged, and all the occupations in which he is successively engaged, contribute every one of them to that general end which he calls life: and what is more than this, that his life is not limited by the satisfaction of his individual needs or the fulfilment of his personal desires, but is itself a part of a life at once higher and wider, to the level of which it is raised, in the amplitude of which it is merged, the common life, that is to say, of his society. And, if rest is a legitimate object for him, a man must interpret it properly; it must be itself an activity of a spirit, well and completely equipped with the fruits of the various detailed occupations which have engrossed him.

Now in a primitive and elementary form of society men certainly were confronted with some difficulties, but by way of compensation may have had some advantages, which are not ours. No doubt when our early ancestors had wrested from the untamed fields or caught in trackless forests the food on which they had to live, when they had with rough implements built their modest dwellings, clothed themselves with the skins of the beasts they had slain, and thrown up rough defences against their enemies, they must have had little leisure for anything but a weary sleep, little opportunity for such rest as we have described. Yet it is remarkable that they found time for waking dreams, for the building not only of houses but of hopes, and it was in these dreams and hopes that they found their encouragement for work and their refuge and their reward. And we may conceive that, hard bestead as they were, they had in one respect the better of us who live in a later time a more complicated life. For, though their needs were urgent and they had little store laid by on which to draw, if on any day their search for food was unsuccessful, and no second line of defence within which to retire from the attacks of an insistent foe, yet these urgent needs were few and simple and the relation of each of them to the supreme need of keeping alive was definite and easily understood.

In a modern community, though little leisure is to be enjoyed by the great majority of those who belong to what are called the working classes, yet it may be fairly claimed that they have a leisure and a security which were not granted to early peoples; and beyond the borders of the working classes there are many individuals and even large groups of persons who have time and energy left over and to spare when they have satisfied the needs of life and done such work as they are called on to do. The average of leisure and the average of security are beyond all question higher with us than with our early ancestors. If we are in this respect in a position superior to theirs, it is not difficult to discover the cause of our advantage; it is that differences of function have been more and more closely adapted to differences of native ability, and that men have devoted themselves with a special and exclusive attention to those activities which they could best perform, and in which they could most readily render to their neighbours services in return for which they would receive those varied rewards which, put together, make up a "living." This specialisation of labour is a natural and indeed inevitable tendency, but, if it has had the result of increasing efficiency along several lines of work, it has also had the result of isolating those who work along one line from their fellow-creatures who work along others. And there is this further consideration to be noted: that, whereas the elementary needs of human life may be said to be always the same, the needs for food and shelter and clothing, yet the progress (and to be sure

the decay also) of civilisation makes men aware of
fresh desires which presently become fresh needs.
Instead of demanding shelter, different men demand
different kinds of shelter or of food or of clothing:
they learn to live more delicately and themselves
become more delicate, and what was sufficient and
good enough for their ancestors is literally neither
sufficient nor good enough for them; they could not
maintain themselves alive with the few and simple
things which sufficed for their predecessors. Accordingly, though our leisure may be greater than that
which men in earlier times enjoyed, both our desires
and our needs are more numerous and more varied.
Though by multitudinous devices of specialised industry we have come to be able to satisfy our needs
without leaving even our desires wholly unsatisfied,
it is much harder for us to relate the special activity
of any individual or the many varied activities of the
many diverse sections of society to one common end.
Yet we postulate a common end in which an individual
may achieve the unity of his own life in harmony with
and in subordination to the unity of a society capable
of embracing both him and his neighbours and in its
fulness transcending each and all of them.

The result is strangely disappointing. The increasing differentiation of the activities of men is to
be justified, if it is to be justified at all, on two
grounds; first, that it will tend to a beautifully articulated co-operation by which all men may be more and
more fully released from merely mechanical labour
and come to be conscious of their mutual dependence

and their corporate unity; and, second, that by allowing individual men to do whatever special work they may have special aptitude for doing they may be able to realise themselves, not only in the leisure which is the fruit and the prize of work, but in the work itself. But the result has been very different from this. Men have learnt, not that they are dependent on one another, but that they are divided from one another, and they have been so wholly engrossed each one, and each group of them, in the routine of their special callings that they have become what we call specialists, people, that is to say, who have learnt to do some one thing with remarkable dexterity and speed, but who are something less than complete and healthy human creatures able to enjoy themselves and the world. But for all this there remains in men a something native and ineradicable, the trembling but persistent belief that they are after all themselves something more than practitioners in various kinds of work, that they make altogether a total common unity which they call society or the state.

This belief, fearfully and doubtfully held, is rarely expressed and then fitfully and with apology; or if there are any who express it loudly they are those who identify their own calling or at best the callings most nearly kindred to their own with the sum of society and therefore find themselves in opposition with others whose voices are as loud as their own, their view being as narrow, who in their turn are determined to identify their own calling or special group of callings with the total. And they are all wrong for a double reason; first because they leave out of their account other callings and groups which actually have their place in the world; and secondly, because they have mistaken the nature of the only total or unity which can properly and effectively embrace men. This effective and proper unity is something more than the sum of what is actual, it is an ideal.

Now it must of course be admitted that all men are more truly idealists than they are generally willing to admit to themselves or to their neighbours; for indeed human life would not be tolerable to the most stupid or the most gross if they were not at times illuminated by the vision of an ideal which, though it pales, is never quite extinguished in their minds. But the difficulty under which they, the stupid and the gross, labour is one which oppresses others also, not stupid or gross but merely timid: and if we add together the stupid, the gross and the timid we shall have accounted for a large proportion of mankind. The difficulty may be simply stated: it is this: all men seek from time to time to escape from the actual into the ideal; but this language is itself misleading, for it indicates, not simply a contrast but a divorce between the actual and the ideal, it suggests a gulf fixed across which there can be no crossing made. The haunting ideal, of course, transcends the actual but is only to be found in the actual, and until it is there sought and found what we call the progress of civilisation will only be another name for the process by which men are divided from each other, and themselves become an ill-assorted conglomeration of diversified interests and aptitudes.

For we cannot but be aware that as there are divisions which separate men from men and groups of men from other groups of men, so there are divisions within a man himself; and just as the divisions which mark off men from their fellows prevent them from becoming all together a single self-conscious society, so these other divisions within the individual prevent him from becoming and realising himself. Speciali-sation, to use a current term, commonly means not the devotion of the whole of a man's powers to some end which is worthy of them and to which he is specially attracted by his special aptitude, an end which might at once satisfy him and enable him to satisfy the claims of a composite but unified society. It means something quite different from this: the exercise and absorption of some particular power or faculty in a man which nature or training or accident has brought to greater strength and a higher develop-ment than his other powers or faculties, and the cultivation of this power or faculty to the neglect of the others.

It may, of course, be said that however exclusively a man may in this latter sense have specialised, the necessities of ordinary human life compel him to engage in more activities than one and therefore to exhibit himself in several, if only a few, rôles. For example, a man may be a dog-fancier or a gas-fitter or a professional politician and may devote himself to

the special work which is indicated by these titles and
yet be obliged, for all his pre-occupation with the
matter which he conceives to be most appropriate to
his distinctive gifts, to play the parts also of a house-
holder, a rate-payer, a father, a son; he may exercise
his special gift and yet cultivate a taste for roses or
for wine, or beguile his leisure with collecting Jacobean
furniture or decorating his drawing-room. And to a
neighbour or a friend who knew indeed what his
special calling was, but was not acquainted with him
merely as a practitioner in that calling he might well
appear to be a man whose life exhibited a remarkable
variety of interests. Even to himself such a man may
appear to be admirable for the range of his own
activities: but if he will contemplate, as from time to
time he is forced to contemplate, himself with a more
critical eye, he may find that what he was proud to
call the range, the variety of his interests is, in fact,
evidence of the confusion and purposelessness of his
life. For he may readily discover that he turns from
his politics or his plumbing or his dog-breeding to the
pruning of his roses and the arrangement of his house
simply by way of escape from the fatigues of those
engrossing avocations, and again that he passes from
one to another of his diversions because he is tired
of each in turn. In each of these several forms of his
varied activity he may become sadly aware that he
is missing what would give to each an enduring
interest and relate each to each. He is, in fact,
missing himself.

Now the self which a man seeks and is ill at ease

until he finds, is something other and more than the sum of the activities in which he is actually engaged or of any other activities which he might substitute for them or add to them; in them he may no doubt strive to express himself; in them he may with lengthening experience and increasing skill learn more and more completely to express himself; or once more he may discover that by changing or diminishing or increasing his activities he comes more perfectly to express himself. But if he hopes ever quite satisfactorily to express himself in these or any other activities, his expectation is foredoomed to disappointment. For himself must always transcend and baffle any form or any number of forms of expression, since form must be definite and the spirit is infinite.

Unwilling to yield unquestioningly to this belief (though unable to free himself from its hold) a man may pretend to be or to have several selves according to the several occupations in which he is successively employed. At home he may be one man, out-of-doors another, with his family a different person from what he is with mere acquaintances and so forth, and he may even pride himself upon his versatility. Just as in the roughly organised group which either prophetically or ironically we call society the grooves or ruts in which men run become so deep that it is difficult for them to look over the edge and see their neighbours, so a man may plough so deeply the divergent furrows along which his varied interests move that it is difficult for him, that partial self which he tries

to identify with one interest, to look over the edge
and find himself, again a partial self which he strives
to identify or to express in another interest. But
though the effort to find the rest of itself may be
difficult for a society, yet men as individuals and as
groups are by nature or destiny driven upon this
attempt. So from time to time we discover that
some fresh formula or system is invented and devised
under which it is hoped to draw together in lively
wholeness the imperfectly related and therefore con-
flicting interests whether of a man or of a society.
Formula succeeds formula, and system displaces
system, and the quest is still pursued but in vain.
A formula is after all a mere label, a system is a mere
arrangement, but what is needed is a principle to
which reference can be made, a law so intimate in its
appeal and so universal in its binding force that
obedience takes the quality of personal loyalty. It
is not the discovery of a new thing that is needed, it
is not enough to lay a new stress or put a fresh
emphasis here or there, it will not help to forge the
links of a chain by which disparate elements in individual or social life are to be held firmly but uncon-
genially together—what is needed is something other
and greater, not a formula or a system or an organisation—it is the spirit of a man or of a society which
is to be discovered.

CHAPTER II

EDUCATION—THE MAKING OF SOCIETY
AND ITS MEMBERS

EDUCATION is the age-long process by which men
and societies of men discover, understand and
take possession of, themselves. This process is not to
be measured only by its length; its range is as wide
as the Universe: it is both the proper occupation and
the final reward of an eternal life.

Education has indeed been defined in other language than this. We may usefully regard it as the
sum of the influences which, converging upon us, have
made us what we are, and are in course of making us
whatever we are to become; more often when we
speak of Education we mean those influences which
are under our control, and which we direct towards
persons who in one sense or another are in our charge;
and sometimes, but more rarely, we mean the influences to which we willingly, and deliberately submit
ourselves.

There is much to be argued in favour of each of
these definitions; the best thing that can be said of
them is, in fact, that they do not conflict any one of
them with the others. But this best thing is unhappily
just what is so seldom said that the truth of it is
commonly forgotten, and so each statement is taken
as a rival to the others, and in competition with them
upheld as though it were complete.

Thus when we say that Education is made up of the sum of the influences which bear upon us, we are apt to set the World and ourselves in contrast; we speak of the World as though it were a great hundred-handed artificer moulding us to its will; or as though it were a river which made its way at last into some hitherto dry and empty cavern, the hollow vacancy of ourselves. But the contrast is not truly drawn, we are ourselves not simply clay in the hands of the potter; it is our hands (though not our hands alone) that fashion the clay; we are not a mere receptacle into which the World pours itself, or as much of itself as we can hold; we are part of the generous and wilful stream; indeed we may more vigorously maintain that, if the World makes us, we make it; if the World gives to us, our gifts to the World are not little or few. This at least we may claim: that if a man is to discover himself, he must in the same act, or as the result of the same series of prolonged efforts, discover also his World. It is in and from his World that he gets his significance; it is from him, as from a centre, that his world spreads itself out in a circle which widens as his self-knowledge becomes more intimate and more effective. For to know himself is for a man to know both his power and his limitations, and his powers are exhibited in operation in the world, in which also they find their boundaries.

In a famous passage Matthew Arnold drew a distinction between a humane and a scientific education: the distinction has been marked less admirably by many persons who unlike Arnold have been reluctant to reconcile the differences between the two. A humane education may quite well be considered to be one in which a man draws his chief and most congenial lessons from the conversation of men and from the records of their achievements in literature or other human documents; and a scientific education one in which he turns more readily, according to his gifts, to the operations of natural forces, which he tries to understand and to subdue. But the record of men's achievement is an account of the efforts they have made to live happily, with their fellows, in the world of external or natural forces; no poet is a stranger to hunger and thirst, to heat and to cold; no philosopher is unaffected by the conditions of his body or the quality of his surroundings. And to study Nature is to essay an intelligible account of Nature, in order that obeying her laws we may become her allies, if not her masters. No man can be so narrow a specialist in either department of inquiry as to be wholly ignorant of, or unmoved by, what is done in the other.

It is, perhaps, too late now to complain of a use of words which is in fact unfortunate and misleading: the study of letters may be scientific; the study of "science" may be humane: it may even be unscientific: it is enough to say that either pursuit is carried on by man for man's purposes, and that neither is followed with advantage if a student arrives at his goal less of a man than he might have been. Yet the specialisation of industry in learning has had precisely this result for large numbers of people. We must see that the great field open to human enquiry is not divided into two departments only. "Humane" studies are themselves divided into many sections; and a man eminent in any one may admit, and will often boast of, his ignorance of others. Thus a philologist may be heard proclaiming that though he "knows" many languages he can speak in none (save his native language, and in that perhaps badly), or a popular or a copious writer may have neither knowledge nor feeling for the structure of language. More remarkable, more monstrous, is the spectacle of literary persons who have no sense of music. Similarly "science" is itself divided into many separate sciences, and each of these into many provinces: chemistry, one is informed, has three or four separate fields, and a worker in one is apt to signalise his proficiency in that by announcing his lack of acquaintance with others. The sum of human knowledge is now so vast that any single section of it surpasses the power and eludes the grasp of any one man, and the whole mocks our struggling imagination.

A man therefore who hopes to attain a useful or even a marketable knowledge of any one department must devote himself to that and quite deliberately accept a large ignorance of other things: he must admit the necessity of forgoing what indeed he cannot attain; he cannot attain a mastery of all that is to be known in every province which the human mind has explored; he can only, and at best, attain a competent understanding of one small section of a single department. To have gone far upon a single track, or in going to and fro upon a short stretch of it, to

have penetrated the surface of a narrow territory to
a considerable depth, a depth at any rate considerable enough to prevent him from looking over the
edge of the entrenchment which his industry has
made, would seem upon this reckoning to be the best
that a painful man can hope for. How then can he
have won the mastery of the world which might seem
a proper goal for ambition untutored by experience
to set for itself? But a more searching question
yet remains—how is it possible for a man who has
followed, as necessity has made him follow, a single
line of investigation, a single kind of work, to reach
that self-mastery which is a conscious realisation of
the variety of his natural powers all fitly exercised,
and all subordinated to a common end? A man who
should gain the whole world and lose his own soul
would be little profited; but that ill-advised barter,
it would appear, is one which he cannot effect. Are
we to say then that he is free to effect the still less
profitable exchange of his own soul, not for the
world, but for a very small part of it?

It is the business of education to solve this problem;
to enable a man to develop his powers harmoniously
and to enjoy a world in which they all have room for
growth and activity. A harmonious development does
not mean an equal development of all his powers—
some one of them is certain to be more lively than
the rest, and some group of them stronger and more
insistent than the remainder. It means the development of them all, the weaker and the stronger alike,
upon a plan orderly and intelligible, so that he is in

the result one man and not a mere name under which disparate and disorderly powers wage an uncertain and a fruitless war. It is clear further that one man will differ from another in the strength, the range, and the variety of his powers—he will exhibit a greater or a less diversity of gifts, and where his neighbour is strong or weak he will be comparatively weak or strong; and however he may differ from his neighbour he will, like his neighbour, be himself, a being whose powers whatever they may be are co-ordinated in such a way that they can be directed to an adequate and clearly conceived end, and together enable him, like his neighbour, to take happy possession of the world.

But the world of which one man takes possession will be a different world from that of his neighbour, or, if there is ground common to both, and indeed there must be, each will enjoy what is common upon a special tenure corresponding with his several powers of appropriation; and for one, or the other, or for both, there will be a margin where he eludes and escapes his neighbour. To be sure, within this margin he will find that he has other co-partners; this will be common ground between him and them, but they in their turn will stretch their dominion over the world in directions in which he is unable to follow them. What results from this is that, while every man may properly be said to have a world which is his own, his world is invaded by his fellows, into whose world he himself makes his way in turn as an invader.

The problem of Education may now be stated in

wider terms—it is to enable a man to become master
of his own world with a secure possession, and at the
same time to make him aware of the other worlds of
other men, identical in part with his own, in spite of
all their differences. In fact, his awareness of his
neighbours, his knowledge of the reality of their
worlds are conditions of his being aware of himself
and of knowing the world which he calls distinctively
his own. Thus we may argue that, even if we regard
education, for convenience to begin with, as the
training of the individual to the mastery of himself
and his world, it is also and at the same time an
undertaking social or political in its character, since
the individual cannot receive this training apart from
his fellows. For, as a man is compact of many powers,
each of which for its just perfection and its proper
work depends upon the harmonious development, the
consonant activity of the others, so a society to be
fully developed and to exercise its manifold and varied
energies demands the contributory services of its
members, each of whom must have achieved humanity
if society itself is to be humane. But society is not
yet humane, its members have not yet achieved humanity, and the business of Education is still to be
done. So we complain, and not without justice; and
we look back, and think regretfully of the long while
that Education has been in process and mourn the
meagre progress made; or we look back again and see
or think we see that once and again in earlier days
something that better deserved to be called a society
than our own existed, and that man in that happy

time had attained a roundness of individual development and a more completely fashioned system of
relationship with each other than we have now.

And here we must state our problem once again
and more fully. Education is to make a man master
of himself and of his own world; to make him aware
of his neighbours and their worlds; and (for this is
what we must now add to what was said earlier), to
teach him and them together to make of all their
several worlds a new, a social, world, a society which
embraces, reconciles and transcends them, and to live
in that new world. What is important to note is that
the new social world cannot embrace and reconcile
the smaller individual worlds unless it transcends
them. Commonly this is forgotten. There are, no
doubt, many who identify education with instruction.
They teach their pupils subjects of which they claim
some knowledge; they do not teach their pupils to
be human, to be themselves. Some of these teachers
of subjects we cannot blame, except for the choice
they have made of a profession; they cannot do more
than they are doing; they know (something of some)
subjects, and they earn a hard living by imparting
what they have hardly acquired. But there are others
who deserve a gentle censure, for they could do much
more than teach subjects; they might spread humanity—or, to be fair, let us say that they do themselves less than justice when they would have us
believe that they are teaching only subjects; for they
love their subjects and are not (for all their shy
affectation) without love for their pupils; they are

better than they know; they do more than they reckon. But they do less than they might do, if they will not admit that at best the subject of which they attempt (with what constant courage!) to give a knowledge to their pupils is a subject of which they must also give their pupils the use. Let them grant so much and at once they must admit further that it is necessary to reflect upon the nature of the use. Of what use is the subject—to themselves, to their pupils, to the world?

The question is not idle. For if a man uses any knowledge he at once brings it into relation with other knowledge which he has; if he uses any knowledge he exercises some power and brings it into relation with his other powers; he becomes freshly aware of himself; and, more than this, his use of his knowledge, his exercise of his power, brings him into relation (whether by conflict, or by alliance) with his fellows and with the world. To ask, then, what is the use of a subject, is to ask what new relationship the possession and exercise of some knowledge or skill will set up within a man and between him and society. In other words, to acquire and to employ new knowledge causes a man at once to go beyond himself, to set up a fresh system of relationship with the world, and to improve or damage the relationships which he has already established. What is true of an individual is true also of a society of individuals. Any activity, any exercise of power, any use of knowledge at once makes it more fully, whether painfully or pleasantly, aware of its constituent members, and also of its membership in a vaster, a more ideal, society. To be sure, the necessity, the possibility of an individual's transcending himself is more quickly seen, more readily assumed; for there, beyond him, and patent to the dullest sight, are other men, of flesh and blood, with whom, in activity, he is brought into contact, co-operation, or quarrel; but, as we have seen, it is not only of them that he becomes newly conscious; he becomes newly conscious of himself, of some total, that is, other and more than the sum of his parts and powers, an ideal, a spiritual self. If we are at a loss to say to what beyond itself a society stretches out when in activity it expands, we may recall what is true of the individual. We may have no name for that larger and more permanent reality to the measure of which he grows; but we have no doubt of it. And if we have no titles, except such as poets have supplied, for that larger and more permanent reality into which society grows, we need and indeed can have as little doubt of it.

Here a problem of very great difficulty and of very subtle fascination awaits us. The larger society of which we have spoken is not the mere dull, or splendid, aggregate of the multitudinous groups or communities in which men have membership, and which together make up the visible state or total society. The larger is also a spiritual society, and it is this, in fact, which gives reality and coherence to the smaller, though large, total society or visible state. The problem is this—at what point of development in the material groups or communities and of the visible state which they compose does it become most easy and natural for a man to realise his membership of the spiritual society, or for the visible state itself to be aware that its wide borders are defined by the surrounding spiritual region? To assume an analogy between the state and the individual is a process which has the support of age and of high authority. Plato has argued from the state to the individual; in the state he saw written in large letters what might presently be descried by trained eyes in the smaller character of the individual. We may argue from the individual to the state, assuming an analogy which may later appear to have some justification.

A man then measures his development by his escape from the boundaries of self. He grows as he learns and fulfils the claims of his family, of the partners of his work, of the members of his party, of his fellow-citizens. So we say; but he grows and he learns these lessons if at each stage of development, which is no doubt marked by his entrance into a larger and more elaborate community of human beings, he passes out of himself in a manner which cannot be estimated or reckoned merely by the increase in the number and variety of his communications with men. He passes out of himself into a higher self, which often eludes his lower or ordinary self, and always escapes his fellows. True, he may remember; true, he may be aware of, this higher self: he will know that it is that which gives significance, outline and unity to the ordinary character which is his: and they will realise that he is what he appears to them to be because he is held in the grasp of a force, not other than himself, and yet higher than the man as they in the dusty traffic of affairs see him. And he and they know, if they care to know, more than this; he and they share the knowledge that it is in virtue of his frequent or rare, but real, passage from his ordinary to his higher self, that he is able to pass from the round of his individual cares and interests into the larger circle of a society's life. And as he moves on with ever widening powers into larger and still larger societies and groups of men, his progress marked by them is measured also, though not perhaps by every eye, by a fresh growth of the higher or spiritual self. Always the condition of real development, of real increase in sympathy and understanding of human affairs, is the widening, the deepening of the spiritual man. Let us grant at once that an ordinary and busy man is seldom aware of what is going on in his own soul; yet from time to time he meets the spiritual reality which is in truth himself; he " comes to himself," and the re-discovery of himself sets him at once in movement to renew and to enlarge his relations with his fellows.

But here a danger awaits him. He may come to identify the growing multitude of his engagements with the growth of his soul. A busy man may become that figure for the satirist, an important person. We see him, note-book in hand, writing down one more in his long list of functions to be performed; he is a member of twenty societies, of a hundred committees, social, philanthropic, political, learned, and

(who can withstand him?) religious. To these he
gives himself. It is a literal account of what he does:
to these he gives himself, and there is nothing left
over. He has forgotten the conditions of real growth;
for it is the incommunicable, but not unfelt, remainder which gives worth to whatever a man may
do in his communication with the world. Without
that, or if that is lost, he is now but a bundle of labels,
a string of titles, and, when his engagements have
been enumerated, all is said that can be said about
him. Had he stopped earlier, had he refused to admit
claims which he could not fulfil except at the price
of his own true life, he might have saved himself and
been of some real, because of some spiritual, service
to his fellows. But no; he had the ambition to be a
"great" man, an "important" person, "a prominent
citizen." Another man might perhaps have done all
that he has done, and not been used up, exhausted,
in the doing; another might beyond the limits of
things done have had a subtle margin of things
dreamed, and beyond that an ampler region in which
no thing could be defined, but in which he himself,
undistraught, lived at home with himself. Such a
man could afford to undertake these countless activities.

Now by every man the decision has to be made for
himself just at what point or line he will set a limit
to his outward engagements and activities, since he
sees that at some point or line he must end them on
peril of his life. And so it may be for societies and
states of men; they, like individuals, have an over-

self, a real or spiritual self, which gives significance and unity to the visible total of their energies and achievements. If their activities are usefully to be extended, it must be on condition that they do not eat their way into that region, which should remain for ever inviolate, of the higher self.

But if it is believed that no limit can be set now, as once limits were set for the sake of clearness and sanity, of intelligibility and self-respect, to the outward and material extension of a state's activities and engagements, then the necessity becomes all the more urgent for making that sacred zone of the spiritual self, which surrounds the visible, ampler and deeper, and keeping it for ever safe from the insidious encroachment or the violent assault of the most alluring or the most clamant of temptations marked as duties.

The business of Education is to give members of a visible state the freedom of the eternal society.

CHAPTER III

AGENTS AND PROCESSES

SPECULATIONS such as we have made in the preceding chapter are often considered and sometimes
expressly called idle by men who claim to be practical.
"If you wish to indulge your fancy," they say to
persons who are occupied with such problems, "if you
choose to spin cobwebs and to pose as philosophers,
so be it: for our part, we must keep the world going,
must see that the world's work is done; we are not
philosophers, but plain men." Let us not delay now
to argue that all philosophers strive to be plain, and
that all plain men have a philosophy original or
adopted. Both are engaging themes, but we shall for
the moment set them aside. Instead of enquiring
what is the meaning of education, we shall now try
to set down some of the things which are done in the
name of education. It will indeed be impossible even
to make a catalogue of these things without indicating
however briefly why they are undertaken; but we
shall pass rapidly over reasons, and record facts as
clearly as we can.

First, then, let us note that in ordinary use education is the general name for certain commodities and
services which men desire, but are not necessarily
concerned to analyse. Thus food is the general name
which covers beef and mutton, cabbages and potatoes;
drink the general name which covers water and milk,

beer and wine; the Post Office or the Ministry of
Health are public services. And these commodities
are supplied, these services rendered by persons and
groups of persons whom the ordinary citizen knows
how to find when he needs what they can sell him or
do for him. He needs food, he needs drink, he needs
the aid of certain national or local services, and he
applies in the proper quarter for satisfaction when
these needs overtake him. Or, since these needs are,
if not continual, at any rate regularly and frequently
recurring, he is happy to know that at any time, if
he can pay the price or prove himself entitled to
receive these commodities and to enjoy these services,
he can get what he wants. The shops are always
there, the offices are always there; he can go to them
when he chooses.

What are the commodities, what are the services,
which men are really seeking when they seek education? We must pause for one moment before we try
to answer this question, and must ask another, which
must first be considered. Are they, these men who
seek education, seeking it for themselves or for others?
A man might seek food; if it were for himself, a beef-
steak might serve; if it were for his infant son, food
in a different form and of another kind would be
appropriate: he might seek drink; if it were for himself, wine might satisfy him; if it were for his child,
water would satisfy him, because it would satisfy the
child; and occasions can readily be imagined when
water would satisfy both him and his child. These
vulgar examples, we hope, make clear certain im-

portant truths—obvious, we should have called them, but for the fact that though indeed, they are in the way so that men trip up over them, they are not always remembered. For it is an important truth that what is food for a grown man may not be food for a child; an important truth also that what is drink for a child may be drink for a man, but not the only kind of drink. There is truth, too, in the old belief that one man's food is another man's poison. With these words of preface and explanation, we may now say that, when grown people seek education they seek it, as a rule and at first for other people, and especially for the young, for their children. They discover the need of educating themselves later, and more rarely.

It is about the education which men seek for their children that we must make our first inquiry. What is it that they expect to get? And, what is of equal moment, what is it that their wives expect to get? The truth is that most men are so much pre-occupied by their business, by the labours which they have to put forth to earn a living for themselves and their families, that they have no time for their children. The men are away at their work from morning till evening, and, when they return to their homes at the end of the day, it *is* the end of the day that they have reached, and with it the end of their energy. They are tired, they are hungry; they need rest, recreation, food and sleep. It is the end of the day, and their children ought to be going or gone to bed. The women are not away from home—not all of them, not most of them, though far too many of them—but they are at work; they are cleaning their homes, cooking, sewing; they are engaged with the feeding and rearing of their babies; they are marketing and planning, and occupied in the perpetual problem of making both ends meet. They have scanty leisure for their children; even for the nursing of their children they have too little time and too little energy; and presently, when necessity no longer compels them to devote such meagre gifts of time and energy as they have to their children, they are caught back by the claims of cleaning, and cooking and sewing, of buying and arranging and acting as stewards and managers of the moneys which their husbands earn. For them, too, the end of the day brings fatigue; they wake only too often in the morning to fatigue which returns with daylight and consciousness.

An answer, then, not the only answer but the first, to our question need not be delayed—when men and women ask for education for their children, they are seeking a safe place where their children can be kept during the day, and trustworthy people who can attend to the children, who will "mind" them during the hours when the parents themselves are unable to take care of them. The place to which the children are sent as soon as they can walk to it must be a safe place: their homes are not safe; they are sent to this place to be in the charge of persons who can take care of them, who will "mind" them: their parents cannot take care of them, cannot mind them. These two implications are irresistible, but they are not often as plainly stated as they ought to be. Facts are facts;

whether they stand to the credit or the discredit of society, they must be acknowledged.

Another fact is to be stated and reckoned with. Children are sent to the safe place, not only because their parents are unable to keep them safe at home, but because the children are unable to take care of themselves. Infancy, the period during which the offspring of men and women are unable to take care of themselves, is longer than the period in which the offspring of other creatures need maternal care. In France there is a name beautiful and terrible for schools in which the children of the poor are "minded." They are called *Écoles maternelles*—schools, that is to say, where the mothers are absent and other women perform the service which mothers might be expected to render. For the majority of people it is necessary to send their children away from home for the working and waking hours of the day. The majority are the poor, or those who, lifted above the threshold of poverty, are yet so tied and bound by the toil either of making a livelihood or of arranging and dispensing the fruits of day-long, week-long, life-long labour as to have no freedom, no time, no strength for watching and guarding their own children.

But this delegation of parental work to persons who are not parents (or are not the parents of those whom they in this manner safeguard) is not dictated by mere necessity, certainly not by economic necessity. For look to the well-to-do and the rich. They cast upon other people the care of their children, and from an earlier age than do the poor or persons of small means. It may not be necessary for the well-to-do and the rich to send their children away from home; but their houses are larger and the children can be sent, banished were perhaps the right word, to a remote wing of the house, or to a nursery in which they will not disturb their parents. Let not the suggestion be made that this habit is due to any laziness or to any incompetence on the part of the parents—or let the suggestion be silenced for the present. The simple explanation is that, let the parents be never so perfectly equipped by disposition and by ability for the care of their children, they cannot do two things at once, they cannot be in two places at the same time. Sometimes indeed they try to achieve what cannot be accomplished; sometimes they are driven upon a sorry and difficult compromise; but for the most part persons who can afford to hire the services of nurses and governesses for their children engage these services because, if they attempted to render them themselves, they would be cut off from the possibility of fulfilling other claims which are made upon their time and their strength. It is of course the woman, the wife and the mother, who is mainly concerned with this problem. Nature and custom both grant to the man, the husband, the father, a large though not a complete emancipation from its dominion, at any rate during the early years of the children's life. What are the rival claims which call the woman from constant attendance on her child or her children? They are the claims of society, the claims of that community of which she and her child are members, but not the only members. And she can only do the best for her child if she also obeys its commands.

Here is a problem which has in it the elements of tragedy. For, if society issues its commands so does the child, so do the children. Both are authorities to be obeyed; but obedience is not easy, since the commands which each issues often are or seem to be opposed to those issued by the other. Society, the community, is a circle with a wide circumference, some parts of which may be faintly and indistinctly drawn, a circumference which may widen, and must naturally widen for persons who themselves continue to grow: a circumference, however, which along certain parts of its edge hardens, so that it becomes a barrier, an obstacle to growth. Within this wide and irregular circumference smaller circles may be traced. The clearest boundary outlines the family itself. The claims of the family and those of the individual members of it should not be irreconcilable; but it is certain that they are hard to reconcile. A child is born into the little world of his family; if he claims and wins the undivided attention of his mother, as he may naturally claim it and is likely enough to win it, he will destroy the group of which he was born to be a member. For his mother owes duties and must discharge the obligations of allegiance not only to the new but also to the older members of her family. A man who gains the presence of a child in his house, but loses the companionship of his wife, may find that his pride in being a father is dearly purchased by his loneliness as a husband. The doubtful eyes with which elder children look upon a new-comer reflect the questioning which disturbs their heart. The circle is enlarged; but what if its comfortable and familiar circumference has been broken past mending? Parents themselves may look wistfully and half-guiltily at their elder children to whom they must give less of their time and their company, though not less of their love, because some of the time (which cannot be lengthened) and some of their company (which is measured, not perfectly, but still with a rough accuracy by the time at their disposal) must henceforward be given to an infant whose rights, whatever else they may be, have not become prescriptive. And, once more, it cannot be forgotten that not only the nurture and rearing of children when they are born cost time and energy, which are two names for life itself, but the making and bearing of children involve a charge upon the same fund.

Now all these claims are claims of the family as it is, and as it grows; and they are hard to square with the claims of its several members. The present has a rival in the past, and is itself rivalled by the future. How are these rival claims to be met? The progress of human society from its earliest forms has provided examples which may be used. Parents must provide themselves and their children with food and shelter and clothing; but they no longer provide these things by the effort of their own hands. They know where to go to buy food; the house in which they live has been built not by them; the clothes they wear and

which they give to their children have been made or
the materials of which they consist have been prepared by other people. The parents still provide
themselves and their children with all these necessary
things; but, on the whole, they provide better because
they call to their assistance other people among whom
these several services of the purveyor of food, of the
builder, and of the clothier have been distributed.
To each of those persons the parents are debtors, they
are under an obligation, which is represented but not
discharged by the payment of money. Directly or
indirectly in return for what is done for them they
must do what they can for other people. They are
not set free from this obligation by the fact of being
parents; on the contrary, it is because they are parents
that they are forced into a more frequent commerce
with the larger world which surrounds the family.
Accordingly it may well appear that, the stronger and
the more numerous the claims of the family, the less
opportunity will there be for the parents and in
especial for the mother to give themselves immediately to their family. Then they must find and
avail themselves of the services of agents who will do
for them what they cannot be present to do themselves for their children. They cannot take care of
their children themselves; they must then put their
children in the care of other people.

How early this transference of children from their
mothers' hands to the hands of other persons should
be made is a question which might be debated did not
practical necessities give it for the majority of people

a quick and definite answer. The children will be sent to places where they can be minded as soon as their legs can carry them, as soon as they can find their way. For the majority the infant school or the infants' department of a school is the place, and to it the children are admitted at four or five or six years of age. Already, indeed, some provision has been made for the care of children even younger, and no doubt ampler and more general provision will presently be made for children who cannot take themselves to school. But the reason for their being sent away is the same, whether they go at three years or at six years of age. Men and women must needs beget and bear their children for themselves; for a short time the children cannot be and therefore are not separated from their mothers; for a short time their mothers are precluded from other occupation; but it is a short time, and then other occupations claim them again, and the children go. They go into the hands of the caretakers.

For whom, it must now be asked, do these caretakers act? Whom do they represent? It is convenient at this stage of our argument to use the title of caretakers rather than that of teachers, though we shall soon find it necessary to adopt the more familiar word, without, however, losing what is implied in the word which for the present we prefer. Surely, it may be answered, it is the parents who are represented by these persons, and for the parents that they act. This is the truth, but it is very far from being the whole truth. We are not here attempting to draw an ideal

arrangement or to sketch a theory; we are attempting
to set down very simply and plainly some facts so
simple and plain that they are rarely named and
probably very rarely noted. The caretakers, the
minders of children, act, not only for the parents,
but for the general society of which parents and
children and caretakers themselves are members.
Custom and law sustain the theory that the children
are not the children of their parents only, but the
children of society. The parents find it convenient
or necessary to put their children into the hands of
caretakers; but custom and law will not have it otherwise, and custom and law speak with the voice and
with the authority of society. An apparent, but not
real, exception is to be remarked in the practice of
the rich or the well-to-do people, who do not make
use of the minding-places and profit by the services
of the caretakers provided and employed by society.
For all alike, rich and poor, sooner or later, and the
rich on the whole sooner and more completely, hand
over their children to other people.

At this point, however, it is worth while to remark
an exception real and not always apparent. The rich
or well-to-do parents can send away their young
children to another part of their own house from that
in which they spend most of their own days and
nights. Presently, to be sure, they will send them to
boarding-schools, but we have now in mind an earlier
stage, when their children can be under the same roof
and yet not *in the way*; and under the parents' roof
they are in the hands of caretakers who are their

parents' servants, nurses, governesses, selected, employed, paid, and, if necessary, dismissed by the
parents. Here, too, it may be said that the children
are the children not only of the parents but also of
society; but society seems to be more remote and
less powerful, the parents nearer and more dominant.
An Englishman's home is his Castle; an Englishman's
wife can choose her own nurse and governess, if she
has the money: we shall later enquire into the reasons
which guide her choice.

We are now concerned, not with the rich who are
few, but with the multitude who are not rich. They
do not select the caretakers for their children, except
in so far as being electors they may have a share in
the appointment of persons who undertake a public
service; the places in which their children are cared
for are separate and remote from their homes, and
differ from their homes in a hundred characteristics,
and not least in the characteristic of being public
and not private; what goes on in these places, the
kind of care bestowed upon their children, the forms
which that care takes, they have very little power to
control or to direct; and the companions which their
children find there are not of the parents' choice,
though the parents may have no dislike or disapproval
for them. We are not here comparing the provision
which the rich make for their own children with
that which the community or society makes for the
children of the majority, with the intention of showing that one is better or worse than the other; and
for the moment the main or the only reason for such

comparison in points of mere fact as we have made is to bring into distinct view the general nature of this provision. Rich and poor alike, and society as a whole, make through their agents provision for taking care of their children. Taking care, as we shall see, is a comprehensive title for all the processes of education. And this provision for the children is made as well on behalf of the parents and of the children as for the benefit of society itself.

CHAPTER IV

NATURE AND DISCIPLINE

WE may now look more closely at this provision and see of what it is made up. When the children begin to go to school they can already walk and talk. They walk with tottering and uncertain step, they talk with a lisping and uncertain voice. They have the experience, the ignorance, the powers and the weaknesses of children of that age. Now care has a negative and a positive sense. Care must be taken of children lest they fall into danger and disaster, and do mischief and injury to themselves and to other persons. Young children have a superfluity of naughtiness which those who mind them need (though they do not always possess) a superfluity of energy to control and to convert into a fund of useful and beneficent strength. For this reason it is a happy necessity by which the earliest and most exacting processes of caretaking are entrusted to women.

It is not the whole business of the caretaker or guardian to say "no" to every desire and impulse of his wards, though it is a real and important part from which he must not be turned aside by the easy seductions of theorists who would have him believe that children must have their own way, and that the office of the teacher is that of a pious onlooker. His task is rather that divine labour of preventing them in all their ways, of anticipating them by a fine

instinct sharpened by the practice of accurate observation and tempered by a philosophy both strict
and generous. He must be beforehand with them,
not so as to take from them the zestful delight of
discovery, but so as to be ready both to interpose
firmly between them and mistakes which would be
too costly to themselves and to the world, and also
to stimulate healthy curiosity and to direct movement. It is also his business to foresee the oncoming
of fatigue, not to stop activity before fatigue has
arrived, but to stop or divert it before it has advanced too far. He must take care, in fact; he must
be a guardian, nicely estimating the resources of
his wards and economically controlling the expendi-
ture of them. He must patiently, but also quickly,
learn their disposition and nature, so as to interpret
them to his wards in activities which are none the
less appropriate, natural, and free because they are
often suggested by him. He must know what they
want, and must know when to tell them what they
want and when to let them find out what they want
for themselves. But, if he is to know what they
want, he must once more "prevent" them; he must
know what they want *before they want it*.

We have already called this a "divine" office. If
the objection be at once raised that it is then not an
office which any human creature can serve, we should
reply that it is better to have a high conception of
guardianship and to admit, when every effort has
been made to overtake its demands, that it still
exceeds our powers, than to have a complete but

petty definition, in which perfection and pride can achieve a sorry success. For it is by stretching out after a remote and lofty ideal that the guardian exercises and augments his own powers, and in that splendid gap between what he can do and what he cannot he leaves room both for the growth of his ward and for the advent of God.

In that uncharted but not unguessed region his pupil and God may meet. When that encounter has been made the pupil feels the shock at once of discovery and of recognition. He learns that this new presence is indeed familiar. The guardian cannot divest himself of responsibility; it is the responsibility of an agent, of one who acts for another; and responsibility is the pledge and token of authority. If the language which has here been used is to be abandoned, if where an earlier generation was content to say God, moderns must use some periphrasis, they may tax their ingenuity to find one that will suit their taste. But they cannot escape the logical force of the theory of education which is contained in the language of the collects, "that we may obtain that which thou dost promise, make us to love that which thou dost command," or "that they may obtain their petition make them to ask such things as shall please thee." To harmonise love with command, freedom with inexorable but welcomed necessity, is the business of the guardian or the educator; and it is not matter for marvel if he has not yet found a solution of a problem in which the infinite is involved and been able to state it in the language of a prospectus or a cookery-book.

The guardian must suggest exercises for the activity of his pupils. They are domesticated, not wild animals. Man, who has tamed the beasts of the field, has put a yoke upon himself. He has brought them into captivity and has put a fence round himself and his kindred. The limitations which he imposes on himself are necessary for his self-conquest and his re-conquest of the world, which was not really his own when (in an imaginary age) he was free to roam in it at large. But just as the horse, now the servant of man, must not only be stabled and fed but exercised, so man, now the master of himself, and intending to be the master of his children in the hope that they one day will acquire self-mastery, must not only be housed and fed but exercised also. The analogy may be pursued. It may be said that the best exercise is work: let the horse be ridden or driven upon some errand which must be done, and he will get his exercise in the journey which has to be taken. But suppose there is no errand to be done, no journey to be taken. He cannot be kept very long in his stable; he must be taken out and exercised, for the sake of being exercised. Otherwise, if his rest in the stable be long, he will be clumsy and fidgety when he begins to work again; and, if the rest be prolonged beyond a very limited period, he will become diseased and incapable either of the exercise which work provides, or of the exercise which takes the place of work. And it may properly be said that before he can take exercise or do work he must first of all be broken in. The aptness and the unsuitability of the analogy are

both useful for our argument. We may admit very
readily that no fair and complete parallel can be
drawn between man and the other animals; yet it
would be folly to throw away such information about
man as may be derived from our knowledge of animals,
and, still worse, to shut our ears to the suggestions
which that knowledge affords.

Most Englishmen are unacquainted with wild
animals; they know at best creatures round which
a ring of human civilisation has been drawn, and
whose ancient rights and liberties of the forest and
the pasture have long been narrowly confined. Yet
from such information as we can get from observing
animals wholly and animals only partially subject to
man, and from comparing them with ourselves, some
valuable conclusions may be drawn. In the first place,
it must be noticed that the creatures which are free
are free to suffer disaster, damage and death, and that
those which have lost their freedom are carefully preserved against damage and disaster, and, if not from
death, at any rate from many of the fiercer pains of
death. A sheep or an ox which is kept in safety—to
fall at last to the butcher—is kept in safety from the
wolf and the tiger. The horse is trained for work and
kept in condition to do his work. For themselves men
have secured some measure of safety and prescribed
a training for work. The concerted labours of men
have had the effect of making every individual in a
community sure of his food—not yet good and sufficient for a really vigorous life for every one, yet good
enough and sufficient to maintain life. Or, if there

are exceptions, as indeed some are reported from time
to time, the rarity accentuates the horror of them.
Let us repeat that we know little of wild animals; let
us remind ourselves that of primitive or natural or
wild man we know probably less: he is a creature of
the constructive and the analytical imagination.

With these provisos, we may now agree that the
vigilance and the energy which wild animals and
primitive men needed to exert in order to maintain
life, domesticated animals and men as we know them
do not now need to exert. Two results probably follow;
first, some of the energy, some of the vigilance, a kind
of brutal cunning, not being needed, cease to exist;
but second, a part of the energy and a part of the
vigilance which were once needed for mere self-pre-
servation are now released, and may be directed into
other channels. They have become, as it were, a
capital, the interest of which may be expended in new
modes of activity—indeed, the capital itself may be
invested in new ventures.

For the lower animals, it has been contended, the
stages of life which precede maturity are stages in
which they practise themselves in the exercises which
they will have to fulfil when maturity is reached.
These exercises are called, by an analogy which is
sometimes illuminating and sometimes quite seriously
misleading, play. Let us grant that a colt when it
jumps and runs "in play" is preparing itself for
jumping and running which will be necessary for it
when it is pursued by a swift and dangerous enemy.
It is strengthening the muscles, developing the agility,

storing up the power of endurance which one day may be needed for saving its life. And again the sportive movements of the young animal may prepare it for the functions to be exercised, at a later time, of reproduction. But two comments have to be made, two cautions noted. The word preparatory is rightly used if it indicates that these activities do in fact make the young animal fit and ready for other activities in which it will presently engage; it is not rightly used if it suggests that either the young creature itself or its parents are of set purpose preparing it for functions which they anticipate, and for which these activities are seen and foreseen to be introductory. And, further, though men who do anticipate what is to come and forecast what they desire may make use of these early activities and turn them to account, it must be noted that, if they profit by the strength and the agility, let us say, of the horse, they employ that strength and that agility for purposes human and not equine. The movements of a saddle-horse or a draught-horse are in one sense prepared for by the gambols of the colt in the paddock, but they are not the same movements as those of the colt. On the contrary, the colt is taught not to do in the service of man what he did in his infantile freedom. The colt is broken in and he is trained to do what without training he would not do. A second nature is imposed upon him, but it is not horse-nature pure and simple, nor horse-nature matured; it is horse-nature instructed and diverted to unhorselike ends by man who uses the horse for his own purposes.

Now the early, extravagant, varied activities of childhood are said to be preparatory to the engagements and tasks of mature human life. The apparent purposelessness of them has persuaded some observers to call them play; the usefulness of them, in fostering strength and producing agility or dexterity or versatility has led the same observers very rightly to set a high value upon them; and when the observers are concerned with education they very naturally go on to argue that the spontaneous, unpremeditated activities of children should be very carefully noted, and that they suggest the proper modes of development, the easiest and safest avenues towards mature efficiency. It is the business of the educator, they say, to watch these activities with a constant, affectionate scrutiny and to follow the lines which they mark out, hastening but not hurrying progress along channels which are shown to be natural.

This is excellent advice, if it is balanced by considerations at which we have hinted and must now clearly state. First, we must recall once again the fact that the human creature is domesticated, not wild (or, as some prefer to say, using a difficult and dangerous word, natural). And consequently on the one hand his earliest activities are already fenced round by limiting conventions; he is not free to play with the fire or drown himself in the brook or to destroy property; his inclination to do these things is curbed; and, on the other hand, the safety which is won for him by the precaution of his elders gives him a margin, a capital of energy, which the wild

animal or the savage cannot store up, since he is
called upon from time to time to run for his life and
to fight for his life. The domesticated animal has the
leisure of the stable, where he would eat his head off
if he were not exercised. The child has the security of
home, in which he becomes rich and over-rich unless
he is taken out to spend in exercise his stored energies.
A comparison between children who are well cared
for and those who are ill cared for makes this point
clearer. The children who live upon the streets and
have early depended upon their wits acquire a sharpness, a quickness which children of the same age
whose lives are guarded and sheltered do not always
possess or exhibit; but they are living on capital, and
their active but impoverished bodies are but too often
representative of their eager but ill-nourished natures.
But the cared-for children may grow fat in mind and
gross in body, if the care which surrounds them is
merely protective; it is good for them to be shielded
from danger, but not too much shielded; it is good
for them to store energy, but energy stored is energy
only potentially useful; it must be spent and used—
The question is how?

It is not unnecessary at the present moment to
remark that the question cannot be answered by the
children themselves. It must be answered for them,
on their behalf, by older persons, their parents and
guardians, by society which uses parents and guardians as its agents. These agents certainly will take
into consideration the nature of the children with
whom they are dealing; but it is not that alone which

they will take into consideration. They will consider
and try to estimate the strength, the character, the
possibilities, and promises of their wards; but they
will not forget that it is in the world that they will
have to live, and that they must be prepared to live
in it. Wishes, clearly formed and articulately expressed, children cannot present for the guidance of
their elders, who will not be unaware that clearly
formed and articulately expressed wishes upon so vast
and vague a matter as their own destiny are rarely
presented even by grown people who have had experience of the world and practice in discovering and
formulating their own desires. The elders will not,
for that matter, be unaware that when grown-up
people have framed and had the courage to express
their wishes in regard to what they themselves should
be, or have, or do, the world is rarely willing to grant
those wishes exactly and fully. Something may be
known and much may yet be learnt about the instincts
of children, their habits may be even more thoroughly
investigated and recorded than they have yet been, and
their guardians may in the light of this information
be able to prescribe for them courses of training more
likely to be fruitful and beneficent than those which
might have been prescribed by other authorities who
lacked the patience and the insight for making these
enquiries or never dreamed that they should be made.

No small or unimportant part of this information
has been gathered by students who have made the
play of children the subject of their sometimes too
laborious research. Certainly the teachers and guar-

dians of children are wise if they try to discover what
play is and carefully note and examine the forms
which play takes. They cannot be mistaken when
they inform us that in the activities of play young
animals and children practise and perfect in advance
activities which in later life they will need for self-
preservation; they cannot be wrong when they bid
us forecast what will one day be necessary from what
is to-day the sportive occupation of rich or reckless
leisure. But they must be willing to take into account
and estimate with impartial justice all the evidence
which they collect, or which can be supplied to
them by unlearned but intelligent nursemaids, elder
brothers and sisters, and even by parents themselves.
They must note that play has its times and seasons,
some forms of play are put aside and others take
their place, and yet others succeed in due season;
they must not claim for childhood on a whole—which
spreads over many rapidly changing stages—a form
or some forms which may be appropriate and natural
to one or some stages of that vague and elastic period.
They must be careful not to stereotype and fix what
is in its origin spontaneous and in its essence fluid and
variable, unless they do so deliberately and of set
purpose. They must not *make* their wards play;
though they may make their wards repeat consciously
what they have previously begun to do without
knowing what they did; they may cause them to
repeat with greater exactitude what earlier and left to
themselves their wards repeated with variations. But
when they have introduced this necessity, this con-

sciousness, this fixity, they must note that they have
exchanged play for work—pleasant work, perhaps;
but work, and not always pleasant. They must remark
not less the conservatism of children than their readiness for change and innovation; they may ring changes
upon games, and may very rightly do this; but when
they have suggested changes and enforced them by
authority with a didactic purpose, excellent as that
purpose may be and necessary as it may well be
proved, again they have substituted for play work—
pleasant work, perhaps; but work, we repeat, and not
always pleasant.

No greater cruelty could be practised upon children
than that which is advocated by some writers of
letting their play provide the map, and mark out the
lines of their training. Much, very much may be
learnt from a careful (and playful) observation of
children's play; but there is no escape from the fact
that, if grown-up people are to concern themselves
at all with children, they must concern themselves
in the way of interference. Responsible for bringing
them into existence, their elders are responsible also
for maintaining them and fitting them to maintain
themselves. The ministrations which a cat bestows
upon her kittens have the effect (and we may, without
much risk of being misunderstood, add, the intention)
of promoting their passage from kittenhood to the
condition of mature cats; they have not the effect of
continuing for them an eternal immaturity. And if
the cat suffers the play of her offspring with exemplary, maternal patience, there are limits to her

endurance: and some forms of their play she will not endure, but summarily check and punish. In particular she will check and punish those forms of play which endanger the lives of her offspring and her own life.

We have so far used the word play, as indeed it is often used, as if it had the same meaning for the lower animals and for children, and again as if it was essentially of the same kind for very young infants and for children who have passed infancy. But though this use is common we shall have to show that it stands in need of correction.

For the present, however, we must leave the problem, and briefly summarise the arguments of the preceding pages. It is clear that children need care, that the care which they need cannot, after very early infancy, be provided for them directly by their own parents; that the services of other persons are accordingly called for; that the care which these persons exercise is partly negative—keeping children out of harm which they might do to themselves or receive from the world, keeping them also from doing injury to other persons. Children must live and let live, and for both purposes a negative care is needed. But they need a positive care also, a care which is directed to increasing their chances of living, to preparing them for living in the world. If it is said that already they are living in the world, the whole problem of education has been briefly and enigmatically stated in those very words. They are living in the world and care is exercised over them to ensure their living more fully and better, that is to say, living otherwise than they now live. The purpose of education is to make a difference, and, though the difference may be decided in consideration of the general aptitude of children and the special aptitudes of the special children with whom any particular caretaker or group of caretakers is concerned, it is not decided by the children themselves; it is decided for them. It is not decided even by the caretakers themselves, except in so far as they are agents for the parents, for the family, for society at large. In their turn, when they have grown up, and already by the subtle, delicate and imperious demands of their own nature (interpreted for them by their elders), the children make and will make decisions for the world; they will make and already make a difference to it; but the active, overt decisions are not now made by them, but on their behalf and not less, but more, on behalf of the world or society itself.

Is it possible to find a word which will conveniently describe the object of these decisions, a word or a sentence? Perhaps the widest and at the same time the most accurate word is "conversation." Children must learn the speech of the world, to hear and understand it, to reply to it; to make advances and to receive answers; to move in the world. At once a very remarkable difference makes itself seen between children and grown-up persons. For children the whole world is open in a sense in which it is not open to their elders. Their elders have received a bias, taken a direction, set out upon a course which with little variation they must pursue. The world is open

to children because neither they nor their guardians
know what course they will take; to the east they
may go or to the west. "As the twig is bent the tree's
inclined." Before the twig is bent, one may say that
it can be bent in any direction; but this wide and
universal choice is only possible before any decision
has been made, and while ignorance invests the future
with a rich uncertainty. Some one direction they
must take, some course they must pursue; and t
choose one is to reject other courses, or at best to make
others subsidiary and subordinate: into tempting
fields they may make rare excursions, when the main
road is for a time left. To the main road they must
sooner or later return. They cannot travel both east-
wards and westwards. Let it be noted that even an
eccentric person has his own main road; he follows
his own devious course and consistently shocks more
ordinary people by his habitual differences from them.

But before the traveller can venture upon any path
he must have some preparation, for in any path he
will be engaged in "conversation"—in dealing with
the world—that part of the world which he will meet
upon it—those other parts of the world which he will
encounter when paths which he does not himself
pursue cut across his own. Some travelling companions he will have, and at halting places, inns and
markets he must needs traffic with other folk.

Parents then, and society, which is the general
parent, bid the caretakers or teachers equip their
charges with whatever they will need, not for com-
pleting their journey but for setting out upon it.

CHAPTER V

CONVERSATION WITH THE WORLD

SPEECH is the key by which we unlock our own minds and make an entrance into the minds of our neighbours. But it is a key which they must have the right to use as well as we ourselves. This image may serve us for a time; we shall presently note the limits of its usefulness.

We are still concerned with matters of fact, with what people do, and though, as we have already shown, it is not possible to divorce practice from theory, we shall try now to set practice first and to arrive at theory when we are forced to read it under pressure of facts of common usage.

We suppose it is true of most children that their earliest speech is learnt from their mothers. Let us suppose that this early speech includes simple sentences in which the most elementary experiences are simply described. The children are hungry, or thirsty, and they learn to announce these facts to their mothers. They desire to go here or there, to take possession of this or that thing, and they can say as much. They can understand something of what is meant by people who have a larger use of language than they themselves have acquired. It is as much as this, but not much more than this that children have for speech when, be their parents rich or poor, they are handed over to persons other than their parents, for that preparation which, it is agreed, they will need for life. The rich and the well-to-do hand over their children to the care of nurses or governesses who live under the parental roof: the poor or the less well-to-do send their children to schools. If the general purpose of education is to enable us to have conversation with the world, the first and the chief purpose is to enable us to have speech with the world.

Now there can be no speech without subjects for speech. If children are to talk, they must talk about something or things. In teaching children to speak we are engaged partly in selecting for them the subjects of discourse, and partly in providing them with language for subjects which they themselves choose or which the world forces upon them. And in learning to speak they learn to discover and to express the relation in which they stand to the world as it confronts them. The world indeed confronts them, but just as at the earliest stage of their life the world is completely represented to them by their mothers, that is to say, that of the world they see and hear nothing but their mothers, who are for them the world, so now the world is represented, not completely but largely, by their teachers. It is as if between the eyes of the child and the world the teacher was held up or posed. That figure blocks the view and also *is* the view, except for a margin happily left over. Beyond the edge, as we may say, of the teacher, the world makes itself seen and felt. But, to begin with, the teacher bulks large, and the world is an inconsiderable fringe or frame in which the teacher is set.

Later, when the eyes of the pupils have learnt to range more widely, the fringe or frame increases in magnitude, and the teacher relatively decreases. Or we may say that the teacher who stood between the pupils and the world becomes transparent, the pupils learn to "see through him," whether because he has proved himself a fraud or because he has proved himself a wise and trustworthy guide. Transparent, we have called him; but colourless he cannot be, unless he will be savourless as well; and if he is savourless, he is useless. But it is not his business to be transparent at first; he must very literally stand between his pupils and the world, which is as much as to say that, again at first and to begin with, he must be to his pupils the world itself.

The nature of our problem forces us to correct every sentence we write upon it. The teacher must be the world to his pupils, but with certain reservations and upon certain conditions. He must, of course, remember what we have already noted, that he does not completely, though he may and must largely block out the large and general world from the view of his pupils in the earliest stages of his dealings with them. He must not forget that though, during the time when his pupils are with him, his part is so large as almost to fill the stage, there is a remainder, longer or shorter, of time when he disappears, if not from the memory yet from the sight of his pupils, and the stage which he occupies is taken by the parents of his pupils. It may well be that when the teacher is present, the parents are remembered, and

that when the parents are present the teacher is
remembered. It may be that the pupils would, if
they could, reject the image that we have used. They
might rather be inclined to describe their experience,
not as that of spectators who look first at one and
then at another actor upon the same stage, but rather
as that of persons who attend now one and now
another theatre—the theatre of school, and that
other theatre of home. In fact we know that, whatever their experience may be, young children at any
rate will not give in set words either of these accounts.
It is older people who, looking back upon their childhood and youth, interpret them by the help of these
images, which may but roughly and most imperfectly
represent what actually befell them in those distant
days; and their interpretation of their own childhood
and youth throws an uncertain and fitful light upon
the experiences of those who are now young.

Yet we may say that the advance from infancy to
childhood and youth is one in which the mind encounters more and more things for which words
become necessary, and more and more words which
need explanation. There is the stage, or there are
the theatres. At first there is one actor, the mother;
presently there are several; at first the actor needs
no language, but makes herself understood, so far as
it is necessary for the child to understand her, by
doing things, and making sounds which need not
even for her be words and for her listener are certainly
less than words. Presently words come to play a part,
or to be instruments in the use of this actor. They

serve to make clear and clearer things which had indeed been known, but less well known without the use of words. But with the increase of words, there is an increase of things or people, to be seen and heard, to whom gradually and perhaps quickly words or names are attached. If we speak of an actor and even call the mother an actor, it must be at first in a very literal sense; she is the person who does things. Yet in the earliest stages of life this actor is not differentiated for the child from himself. She, to be sure, in acting for him must sever herself, in imagination, in understanding, and even in physical difference from him; but for him she is not at first an actor even in this sense. She is not so much one who acts for him as one who acts with him. Or we say, perhaps, more accurately that there is a unity in which the action of each and the corresponding, balancing, action of the other are the conditions of a common life. Where there is perfect consonance, there is no need for words, and silence enshrines a complete harmony.

This harmony is disturbed, this consonance broken by a necessity in the life both of the mother and of the child. It is the necessity of growth. And growth is extension beyond the confines of an environment congenial and perfectly adapted to the growing creature into an environment which is not, though it may become, congenial and even perfectly adapted. Conversation means turning round in the world, presenting a fresh face to its new and varying aspects, making a home of it, turning its unfamiliarity into conditions of use. But if growth is a law of life, or, to put it more simply, if living creatures cannot help growing, then the fact of growth involves the necessity of exploration, extension into an ever enlarging world. But the world itself grows beneath eyes which learn to see more of it and more in it. And, though this twofold process of learning, the extensive and the intensive, is better described by the general word conversation than by the word speech, there can be no question that the process is aided by and in part identical with the acquisition of a speech which becomes continually wider in its range, and more exact in its significance. We may put into the mouth of children two questions: they ask in fact, though not always and not at first in express language, "What is this new thing with which, as it seems, I am now brought into touch?" They ask also "What is this, apparently, familiar thing, with which I am now brought into a new and strange relationship?" Both questions are provoked by a sense of discomfort. And the discomfort will continue until the new thing or the new relationship is adjusted to the sum of old things, or to the sum of familiar relationships. The world is being enlarged for the child from day to day by fresh additions which must be absorbed and fitted into the experiences previously gathered.

It is also being broken up into new divisions as the eyes which behold it become more critical. The process of addition and that of analysis would be merely confusing if they were not and so far as they are not accompanied or immediately followed by a process of reconstruction or redintegration. Now the double operation of analysis and synthesis which the mind directs upon the world is a process which it directs at the same time upon itself. "There is, then, in psychology as in biology, what may be called a principle of 'progressive' differentiation or specialisation[1]." But this differentiation, this specialisation within the mind must be like those processes which the world accepts from the mind; we almost may go so far as to say that they are identical. The mind becoming aware of new things in the world, and new relationships which it must hold to things long familiar, becomes at the same time aware of new elements in itself, of new aspects or powers. Now newness is strangeness and strangeness is awkwardness, and awkwardness is the enemy of conversation. The mind which is to be at home in the world is a mind which must be at one with itself. If it is to have speech with the world it must have speech with itself.

We now reach a critical stage in the caretaker's or teacher's duty. Earlier it was his duty to stand between the world and his pupil; now it is his duty to introduce his pupil to the world and to bring the world to his pupil. When the mother, the nurse, the governess more or less completely blocked the vision of the child, yet beyond the margin of these persons' influence the world loomed upon the untrained eye, and shone with so bright a light as to make them in a measure luminous: now, conversely, when it is their business to bring the pupils into relation with the world, they cannot do away with themselves,

[1] Cf. Ward, *Psychological Principles*, p. 50.

their personality must be taken into account, their
quality and character cannot but give colour to the
world of which they are the interpreters. Let it be
granted at once that the professional interpreters are
not the only interpreters of the world; yet the fact
remains that certain persons are specially engaged
for the task. And they can only interpret so much of
the world as they know.

And what is their office? Their business is to
conduct speech between the world and their pupils;
the world and the pupils are as it were the principals
at a conference; the interpreter must make them intelligible, each party to the other. But here our
metaphor becomes distractingly interesting. For, first
of all, if the world and the principals are present,
nothing can be absent, not even a subject for speech.
Whatever speech is held must be about the world and
about the pupils. And secondly, if the world is present,
the pupils cannot be an addition to the world; more
than all there cannot be; the pupils therefore must
be a part of the world. We may add, for the same
reason, that the interpreters are a part of the same
world. And lastly, it is now clear that whatever speech
goes forward is the speech of the world with the world,
of the pupils with the pupils, of a self with a self.

If it is argued that such speech as we have described
is perfect and complete speech and therefore not to
be compassed by beginners or even by more practised
speakers in an imperfect world, we shall readily agree.
Yet this ideal of a perfect and complete speech is of
value as a standard by which imperfection may be

tested and progress recorded. It stands as a warning against a very grave danger. The danger is that in teaching speech and introducing children by speech to the subjects of speech, we may establish in their minds a mistake common enough in our own minds of figuring the speaker, the listener, and the matter about which they talk as three separate elements, each of them outside of the others. This figure it is not unnatural for teachers and their pupils to fashion, and at an early stage it may represent a part of the truth. But the object of speech is to effect a unity between speaker, listener and subject, and as soon as this unity has been really attained both speaker and listener discover that they have not so much made a unity as revealed to themselves a unity which already existed, but of which they had been unaware. The world in fact always embraced speaker, listener and subject, and the effect of speech has been to analyse an inarticulate unity into its constituent parts, not by the severance of part from part, which would bring about their destruction, but by a process of intelligent and conscious synthesis; that is, the putting together in the mind of elements which were already together, though their alliance had not been detected.

As we have already admitted, to teach children (or older persons) to speak is to provide them with the subjects of speech. These subjects are a multitude which none can number, and such store of them as any man can acquire may both perplex and burden him, if he regards each one as a fresh and separate possession, a monument of his own skill and patience

and resource. He may acquire subjects as the vulgar
rich acquire pictures, or chairs or horses or objects
of art, and discover sooner or later that he has been
a fool for his pains, since a man's life consists not
in the multitude of the things which he possesses.
Things, reckoned as possessions, take a quick ven-
geance upon the man who claims to own them, for
they take possession of him, and quarrel over their
distracted and dismembered prey. Things reckoned
as instruments are no longer mere possessions, they
have already become parts of life itself; tools of which
the mastery has been won are like limbs of the body
or powers of the mind; they have been brought into
relation with each other by being subordinated, all
of them to a single, if a many-sided and versatile,
personality.

It may indeed be said that possession is only
justified when the things possessed, whether they
be material or spiritual, whether they are bricks and
mortar or knowledge, have ceased to be possessions,
and have been absorbed in the life and taken their
place in its general fabric. But, though the statement
is true and has its use, we have to remember that
possession in this sense is a high accomplishment
which a man will have done well if he acquire in the
course of a long lifetime. And there have never been
wanting moralists who, realising clearly how much
possessions may let and hinder men, have advised
their fellows to get rid of their wealth as quickly as
possible and to live the simple life. Some of these
teachers have even been willing to attempt to put

their own doctrine into practice. They deserve our
praise for their courage and their sincerity; but
success they cannot have. All great maxims are
oracular and need interpretation from a casuistry
which unites reverence with common sense. Those
are true words which declare that we come naked
into the world and naked depart from it. But he
would be a poor commentator who should urge men
quite literally to accept them. However they go out
of it, men ·come into the world to find themselves
already the heirs of a wealth which they have not
themselves amassed, though they have yet to learn
how to use any or all of it. They must set their hands
upon it piecemeal, taking up this and then that good
or bad thing which has been bequeathed to them and
making it in some sort their own. But let us for a
moment pretend that the great saying justly de-
scribes men as they are at birth. What is certain is
that they cannot help acquiring many things, and
that they must acquire many things in order to make
the journey, whether it be long or short and with
whatever fortunes it may be attended, between birth
and death. If they come with nothing (which is not
true) and go with nothing (which is most improbable),
there is no question that between coming and going
they must have many things. Let us not forget, what
has already been more than once repeated, that really
to have, properly to possess, is to have drawn the
thing "possessed" into life, so that it ceases to be a
thing and is become a part of him who has it, as inseparable from him as his hand, as inalienable from

him as his thought. Let us not forget this, and we shall quickly see that before men have learnt properly to possess they may be expected improperly, imperfectly to possess. We may have some patience with ourselves and with our neighbours if we and they learn a hard lesson by many slow and perhaps painful stages. We may learn to be very tolerant without turning our backs upon our ideal of *conversation*.

And we may at this point put to ourselves some practical questions. What are the things, the possessions, the knowledges, which we believe that every human creature ought to acquire, and sooner or later to absorb into his being and nature, in order that he may deserve the place which by birth he inherits as an ordinary citizen or member of the world? And again, since every man may be said to belong not merely and not so much to the whole world as to some special section of it, what are those other things which he ought to have in order to deserve and to keep his place in that special section? And last, since every man is in some sense extra-ordinary, alone in the world, alone even in his own section, what are the things (we still use that most general word) which he ought to have in order to be satisfactory to himself? These are hard questions, and a severe condition is laid upon those who try to answer them. The condition is this—the answer to any one of these questions must be reconciled with the answer to the others. Is a man "alone in the world"? Even his loneliness must be a relation in which he stands to it. Is a man a member of some special group? Then he must fulfil his obligations to it without losing his unique and individual quality, and without forgetting or disclaiming his place in the larger whole? Is he a "citizen of the world"? That great title must not absolve him from allegiance to his special section of the world or from loyalty to his own nature.

He who is able to harmonise these claims is the educated man; the measure in which any man is able to harmonise them is the measure of his education: the measure of his failure in any one of them is the measure of his failure in all. This is an ancient doctrine, but it has not lost its vigour or its value. When Plato claimed that the guardian should be a man who neither feared death for himself, nor lamented the death of a friend "as if some fearful thing had befallen him," he went on to "affirm this too, that such an one is pre-eminently sufficing to himself in living well, and is least of all men dependent upon others[1]." But the self-sufficing man is no selfish miser of a cloistered virtue. He is to be put to many tests to prove his fitness to take and fulfil his part in a community; he will have learned the justice which consists in every man's minding his own business, and "being a good guardian of himself and of the music which he was taught, and showing himself in all these matters to have an orderly and courageous character ...he will be most profitable both to himself and to the commonwealth[2]."

We have already shown that neither parents on the

[1] *Rep.* III, 387 D, E.   [2] *Ibid.* 413 E.

one hand nor the community as a whole on the other can shake off their share of responsibility for the preparation of the young for the life which awaits them: yet a special, if a delegated, responsibility rests upon the caretakers, as we have called those persons to whom parents and community both entrust their children. We may now state the nature and the scope of this responsibility more exactly. It is the duty of these persons to equip their charges with such knowledge and skill and to train them in such abilities and aptitudes as will give them the right of entry into the large world and the right of re-entry into their own spirits. Into the whole of the large world evidently their pupils cannot enter; but the teachers cannot foretell with any certainty along what avenues in the world, along which of its beaten tracks, or through which of its untried regions they will make a way, of their own choice or under the stress of necessity or by that combination of forces in which their native impulse and the pressure of the world unite to carry them along a resultant path. But something they do know: they know that wherever fortune and force lead their pupils they must hold conversation with other human beings and with themselves, and they must help them to take up and carry on this conversation. Now there can be no conversation unless those who are to be parties to it are aware of each other, have the means or the instruments for communication and some matters which they can communicate.

CHAPTER VI

LIFE AND LANGUAGE

THE business of the teacher is thus to make his pupil aware of the world. If it is said that the child is already aware of the world before he comes under the direction of a teacher, there is no need either to quarrel with the statement or to suppose that it removes and cancels the office of the teacher. The child has life itself before he comes to any teacher, but it is the business of the teacher to see that he gets life more abundantly. So it is for the teacher both to deepen and to widen his pupils' knowledge of the world. And this knowledge is gained by exchange. The word commerce may be used for our present purpose. There is a commerce of ideas, as well as a commerce of material commodities. To be sure, some things are bought without money and without price; their value is not to be reckoned in any coinage; but these things are of so vital a necessity that they are properly likened to life itself, and we may justly say that they are won by exchange; we pay with life for what we live on. Yet life is never seen; it escapes detection and definition like the soul; it hides itself behind and reveals itself in things and outward activities, and these are named and expressed and explained in words.

If, then, there is to be any conversation between the pupil and the world, and if there is to be a growing

conversation, the teacher must help the pupil to
understand that he has some things about which he
may talk to the world, with which he may do business
with the world, and that on the other hand the world
has things about which he may listen to its speech,
and which he may acquire in exchange for what he
has to give. The first task of the teacher therefore,
when the child is come to the stage at which speech
begins, is to bring him into acquaintance with those
things which already he shares with the world, and
which he will continue to share with it, whatever his
own special course of development may be. This
business may be described in other words; it is the
work of making the child see and understand that
the very things about which he is himself most
intimately and most constantly concerned also intimately and constantly concern the world itself.

We have used the word "things" and we have used
the word "activities"; both are necessary for our
purpose. The child feels and does things; he sees, he
hears, he tastes, he smells, he touches; and if we reflect
upon each one of these feelings we cannot but observe
that in each or through each either he may receive a
communication from the world or convey one to it;
to look more closely into the problem is indeed to
remark that he does both of these things at once, he
both receives and conveys a message. But the message
of mere sensation and response does not satisfy him;
he desires about some of his feelings to be more precise; not only to have them, but to say what they
are, and by saying what they are to arrest them and

to perpetuate them; he must receive and analyse what he receives; he must act and act consciously. But when he does all this, when he delays and lingers upon his feelings and his activities, he is aware of what he is doing; he is seizing with a firm and a firmer hand the things which he touched; he exercises each of his senses, not for the sake of exercising it (*that* is, as it were, thrown into the bargain) but in order to catch and keep something—the scent of a flower, the savour of a food, the sound of a voice, the form of some object on which his eyes rest. Things he makes his own; he discovers presently that, in capturing things, he has made two captives besides; he has laid hold of the world and he has laid hold of himself. And now he is on the eve of a further and a greater discovery. These things, real before, become now spiritually significant; they are aspects of himself and of the world, modes in which he and the world express their life; and the clearness and fulness of his speech about these things gives him knowledge of himself and of the world, in which he now consciously lives, but which hitherto was only some other, over against himself.

The subject matter for speech, for the conversation held between the individual and the world, is then nothing but the individual himself and the world itself. The truth is veiled by necessity and by decency. It is not good manners to talk about oneself; and it is only possible for a philosopher to talk about "the self." Common folk talk about you and me, and yet, with a certain pleasant reserve, which happily permits a fulness and freedom of speech which would else be unpleasant or beyond compassing. Common folk talk about the things which they have in common. And the world is populated with common folk, who talk about common things, because they have too little philosophy and too much propriety to talk overtly about themselves or "the self."

We must, then, assist our pupils to discover and to name these common things which they share with the rest of the world; for it is through knowledge of these things, or under the semblance of knowledge of these things that they will come to know both themselves and the world. What are these common things? What else, but eating and drinking, and things to eat and to drink; clothing and shelter; heat and cold, the progress of the seasons, the alternation of day and night? What else but the sun seen in the day, the moon and the stars by night; clouds and storms, and streams and rivers, making their way from hidden springs, from high places in hills and mountains to the valleys and the plains and onward to the sea, the fishes of the water, the birds of the air, the beasts of the field? These are the common things, and men move in the midst of them, observing and taking note of all, seeking some, escaping from others as well as they may, and striving deliberately or learning by happy chance and not less by misfortune to adapt themselves to these things or to bend them to their purpose.

Upon the earth man moves, surveys it, guesses at its hidden treasures, and forces it to release its secrets; upon the water he ventures, and loses one land to find another; he meditates flight in the air; he matches his strength against that of the beasts, and, since he cannot rival them, he does more, he tames them. He encounters his fellows, and establishes customs and makes laws, rules of speech and of conduct. Death he confronts, and is not daunted. These are the common things which every man shares with every other; to these the child is introduced when he is born; these are forces which smite upon or caress his senses, which fill his imagination, from which he cannot sever himself, but by which he would be overwhelmed if he did not learn speech, the art of articulate words and co-ordinating thought, the art of conversation, of conducting himself in this crowd. From the crowd he must disengage himself, if he is to learn how much he has in common with it: the crowd itself he must sort out and disentangle if he is to learn sympathy with the human creatures like himself who are part of it: from himself he must separate them in order to perceive his oneness with them; and he must separate them also from the scene in which they and he move, if he is to perceive at last how this creature of the dust, which is man, is by the creative power of human imagination, made the maker of that from which he springs. These things, and the emotions which they stir, the thoughts which they prompt are our common inheritance; to move through these things is our curriculum—drawn, not by the pen of a schoolmaster, but by that of nature herself. We enter upon our inheritance when we enter upon life, for life itself is the inheritance.

It is the business of the teacher to assist his pupil to make good his title, to make effective his potential possession of the world. He can only do his business if he remembers that he is himself a part of the world with which he desires his pupil to have clear and intelligent conversation, and if he presents himself to his pupil as one of the elements of that world, as natural as the sun, though less brilliant, as natural as a stream, though less limpid, but always natural, one of the objects of the child's own natural curiosity. The arrival of the schoolmaster should be very quiet and unostentatious, or, better still, he should not arrive, he should be there and discovered in his setting; and his general setting is the large world in which the pupil is himself placed and as by a happy coincidence also discovered. It is not for the schoolmaster (or other teachers) to interrupt the reverie of the child who scans the broad world, and looks into the vast heaven; it is for him to add understanding to inquiry in such a sort as forever to widen the range of both. He should be the ready and willing victim of questions; the source of explanations; he should offer, but not too publicly, a hand when his pupil needs help in passing over difficult ground. He must have the manner of a fellow traveller, whose path has hit upon that of his pupil, and he should have this manner, not as an accomplishment merely, but also because it very exactly represents the fact. Such he should appear, because such he should be. He should have the manner moreover, of a man who, having fallen in with, being overtaken by, or having himself overtaken another upon a road or in a path, knows that presently his course will carry him away from his companion. For the time they are together; the older person has moved along this part of the journey before, but it remains new to him; he remarks with chastened and practised curiosity things which had escaped him before, or which are indeed now newly to be seen in this road; he recognises what he had earlier observed. He answers questions, when he is asked; but his main comment is unspoken, though not unnoticed by his companion, who has eyes to see what this other, this elder, person is doing, and to remark what effect the world, this piece of the world, has upon him.

Such speech as they have together will be mainly held about the path in which they are moving, or about the objects which are near to it. Through the great world they are moving, it is true; but they are moving through it because they are moving over this part of it and along this particular way. They may pause sometimes, silently to contemplate the large surrounding territory, to look up into the sky; but they must not pause too long. The journey is to be made; and why? Because at the end of it, or at the end of the stage, both travellers are expected; they must not fail those who are looking for them; something they must bring in their hands, the wages of labour; something in their minds, news of the world, the record of their journeying; not empty-handed, nor with empty minds must they come; they must not disappoint their friends. But pause they

must from time to time; and the reverie will fall on
both, and both again, but the elder first (if he be a
fit teacher and have gained in life as he has gained
in years) must be pricked and seized and pierced by
curiosity once more, by wonder large and vague, and
by wonder specially directed to some special thing.
The good teacher sets an example of concentration
and also of relaxation; his attention is now narrowly
focussed, and now his mind, like his eye, roams widely.

It is clear now that when we speak of conversation
we mean not indeed two irreconcilable tasks, but two
activities of which one has a narrower and the other
a wider range and province. The pupil, like his
teacher, belongs specially to some place and some
time, the place and time in which he is born and from
which he sets out; he has immediate neighbours and
surroundings; but he is also set in the infinite universe
and his years are part of an eternity; he must learn
to converse in both provinces. The interest and value
of his conversation with those who are at first nearest
to him and with whose lot his own is most closely
bound up depend very much upon the frequency,
and the length, of his adventurous expeditions into
the wider province; the interest and value of his conversation there depend very much upon the intimacy and vividness of his relationship with those to
whom he is most closely allied by birth and by the
links of early inheritance and tradition. Unless he
makes excursions, if he always stays at home, he will
be very dull company for those who have to live with
him; if he will never live at home, he can never be

a real man; when he makes his way abroad, he will only be a wraith, a simulacrum. And he must live at home, in a jealous isolation, within himself; to himself he must learn to speak, to himself he must listen; and the rule is stringent here also; if he will live only with himself, he will be dull company for himself; if he will never live with himself, he will have no substance, no reality on which his neighbours can seize. An individual he must be, a recluse; but not less must he be a citizen of the world.

Objection may be raised here by critics who should say that "citizen of the world" is a title of pleasant sound but of no clear meaning. The world, they may very properly say, is too big for any man to make his own; along some very narrow track he must walk, and for no very long distance; so much and no more is allotted to him, and within that province he must not only live, but in order to live he must even earn his living. All this is truly said, but it is not an objection to the claims which we have set up. The reply is very simple and can be quickly made: unless a man will fulfil the duties of his special and very narrowly limited sphere, he cannot be a citizen of the world, because he cannot be anything at all. But he can look out beyond the confines of his special sphere; he can enjoy holidays; he can make excursions; and even if he stands still and listens and looks, all those things of which we spoke are his to contemplate, to question, to appropriate and to enjoy. And a main reason, though not the only reason, for his stretching out in imagination and in actual adventure beyond his own plot of the earth is that unless he does this he cannot come into communication with his fellow men.

Here we have the word which we earlier used—communication; for that he must have a heart of sympathy, the instinct of sociability, it is true; but he must also possess the instrument of communication and, above all, matter to communicate. Now the subject matter for communication consists of those things which we named. Those things he apprehends from his own standpoint; those same things other men apprehend from theirs. Among men there may be some who, if we trust Wordsworth, have a special sensibility for these common things; on their lips common words, set in an order uncommon only because of its perfect propriety and fitted with a rare aptness to the things which they represent, may take on a special significance with a singular beauty. But the subject matter for poets and for ploughboys is drawn from the same world; it is the subject matter of daily commonplace experience. Some parts of the vast field of experience must necessarily be more familiar than others to any man; some parts of it again a man must of necessity learn to deal with more quickly and more certainly than with others; upon his dealing with some parts his living depends. But, if he must be careful in walking along a street at night not to strike against a lamp-post, it is not for us to say that he must abandon the habit of star-gazing. If he must attend to what is going on under his very nose, it is not for us to say

that a breeze blowing from very pleasant places afar
may not quicken his sense.

Teachers must, to be sure, according to their
capacity, help their pupils to fasten firmly upon the
business of the moment and of the place in which
they live; but not so firmly as to become literally
absorbed in it and identified with it. They must
themselves play other and larger parts than those
assigned to them by their professions, narrowly and
strictly defined. Too often they are taken by their
pupils to be "teachers" and no more. They should
present themselves as men who happen to be teachers.
Too often they are regarded as animated subjects;
one saying "I am Geography" and another "I am
Mathematics." But men are better and bigger than
subjects, and should not conceal their quality and
their size too studiously and too long, lest the fearful
nemesis befall them of becoming what with a mis-
guided professional enthusiasm they have for years
pretended or boasted to be.

The danger does not beset teachers only; it lurks
in waiting for all men who have any special function,
even those who are dilettanti of nothing in particular.
Men learn the jargon of their trade and speak to
those who use it about their trade and that only;
they are eaten up by the thing which gives them
bread and butter. "Hence it comes," says Mr Leacock[1], "that insurance men mingle with insurance
men, liquor men, if one may use the term without
after-thought, with liquor men: what looks like a

[1] *Essays and Literary Studies: The Apology of a Professor*, p. 13.

lunch between three men at a club is really a cigar having lunch with a couple of plugs of tobacco." It were idle to argue that a man is absolved from the necessity of spending most of his time at that one thing or that small group of things, his work upon which is his contribution (little or great) to the general wealth of the world. That may and must be granted; but it is not necessary for him to spend the whole of himself upon that thing or those few things. He must keep a margin inviolate, a balance untouched; he must be able to call his soul his own. Of specialisation there is no end; the man who devotes himself to one thing, will presently devote himself to a part of that thing and then to a fragment of that part. "The truth is," to cite Mr Leacock again, "that a modern professor for commercial purposes doesn't know anything. He only knows parts of things[1]."

It is not only the "professor" who falls under this indictment; but, if we bring other specialists under it, we must not forget that it falls only too often upon the teacher. He deals only with parts of things; he is concerned only with a shrinking plot picked by caprice or chance out of the universe; for the centre of that he makes his blinkered way; if he ever tried to trace its boundary, he might discover that he had begun to define the world itself. It is worth while to ask an easy question—Why do children relish the large discourse of an old nurse or a gardener more than the lessons of their "teachers"? Our answer

[1] *Op. cit.* p. 30.

certainly is that the discourse of these persons *is* large. It may be inaccurate; but it leads on and outwards from one thing to another. The teacher is afraid of trespassing on another teacher's land. But without trespass there would never be exploration, annexation, conquest—and very little conversation. And to any lovers of peace who are affronted at these words which have the savour and suggestion of warfare, it must be a sufficient reply that the strife which we have hinted at is really internecine; the antagonists eat each other (as children say) quite up, so that nothing is left of them, except a memory incarnate at last in a society.

We may now set out the elements, the subjects, the stages of the great curriculum in the language of a poet[1]:

Many a wonder walks the earth, but wondrous
  None is as Man: across the sea foam-white
Driven by the storm-blast, plunging through the thund'rous
  Chasms of surge, he wings his aweless flight;
Layeth his grasp on Earth, supreme, undying
  Mother of Gods, and ever year by year
To and fro pass his ploughs; the steed's sons plying
  Ever her stubborn strength, outweary her.

Yea, and the airy-hearted birds he snareth,
  Trappeth the savage prowlers of the wold,
Takes the brine-haunters whom the deep sea beareth
  In his net-meshes—Man the cunning-souled;
Quelleth the forest-crouching, mountain-roaming
  Monsters by his devices masterful,
Bridles the stormy-maned, indignant-foaming
  Horses, and yokes the tireless mountain-bull.

  [1] Sophocles, *Antigone*, 332 *seq*, trans. A. S. Way.

Speech hath he taught himself, and thought swift-flying
    Windlike, all instincts which the state maintain;
Shelter from frost he hath found, from cheerless lying
    Under the bleak sky, and from arrowy rain.
Ever resourceful, found in nought resourceless,
    Dauntless he meets the future's mysteries:
Helpless against Death only, the remorseless,
    His cunning foileth desperate maladies.

Crafty inventions, subtle past believing,
    Now unto evil bring him, now to good.
When he hath honoured Law, by oath receiving
    Justice's yoke, proudly his state hath stood.
He is an outcast, whose presumptuous daring
    Moves him to be with sin confederate bound:
Never abiding by my hearth, nor sharing
    Thoughts of my soul, be such transgressor found!

CHAPTER VII

SUBJECTS OF DISCOURSE

IF men make their gods in their own likeness, they cannot accept for themselves limitations which they would scorn to impose upon their divine creatures. "The earth is the Lord's, and the fulness thereof; the world, and they that dwell therein." This is the infinite field of human speculation because it is also the home in which men live. Within it men have made for themselves a partner, from whom they cannot be divorced, they have got an inmate, whom they cannot put out. They may assign to Him the fulness of the earth, they may say that the earth is His and all its inhabitants; but He is theirs. Themselves and yet not themselves, He is forever present and remote, revealed and hidden from them. He is the form in which they apprehend the world, in which they find or seek an intelligible unity in the confusing world which through Him they claim. He is the hypothesis on which they trust both for the coherency of their speech and for the rationality of their conduct. He is the vital condition upon which they must rely if their speculation is to go beyond the vague scanning of an unmeasured sky or an aimless wandering over a boundless earth, and become sight and understanding, and if the home in which they live is to deserve its name by falling for them into ordered arrangement. He is what they need,—a boundary;

and, what they need not less, a boundary which moves and grows into an ever-widening horizon. If they are to have their world and dwell in it with content, they must come to an understanding with the God whom they have "made."

If there is any truth in the paragraph which has just now been written, it is clear that wide and long as was the "curriculum" which was drawn in the preceding chapter it must now be made larger still. Men must give to themselves some account of experience, they must interpret the world, they must not only possess, but, having called into their world a God, must recreate, the world which they possess, to become a place of habitation for Him as well as for themselves. This might have been put into philosophical language, or indeed into several varieties of philosophical language. Religious language has been used here for three reasons; first, because it is at once more vivid and more general, and, second, because in fact philosophical enquiry, or at any rate that sort of philosophical enquiry which men have attempted in the hope of grasping the sum of things and regarding Reality as a whole, would seem to have had its origin and sprung from religious meditation[1].

To have said this, it may now be argued, is to have gone even further than we went in the last chapter and to have gone altogether too far. Can it seriously be contended, the question will be asked, that the student of education is to range so widely, and that every child is to be considered not only free to wander

---

[1] Cf. Webb, *God and Personality*, p. 139.

in, but bound to explore this vast domain, that he is
to learn to converse with the world, with man and
with God? The reply, sufficient for the present is,
that, nothing less than this can properly be claimed;
that any selection from this total would be artificial
and for our main purpose, that of understanding ourselves and our environment, disastrous, since we
cannot attain the unity of view and the order of
arrangement which we desire unless we hold within
our view whatever the prospect offers and unless we
draw into our system of arrangement whatever the
mind has conceived. And these words which we have
used, man, the world, God, stand for what men have,
however variously and imperfectly, yet fashioned in
imagination, recognised in experience and embodied
in language itself.

We have used the word "curriculum": it may
suggest to our minds the image of a course, a race-
course, indeed, marked out and fenced; a course on
which no ordinary traffic is suffered to move, and on
which only for exercise or for display specially selected
creatures, carefully bred and judiciously trained, run
under the eyes of owners, experts and bookmakers,
who are conspicuous in a crowd of habitual idlers or
of revellers who enjoy an occasional holiday. Such
a race-course has its uses, not the least of which is
found in the pleasure which it affords to that large
company of spectators whom we last named. The
word curriculum, used as it is more frequently in a
narrower sense, calls to our minds the training itself;
and the stages and methods of the training, through

which the competitors are made to pass in preparation for the day of trial. There is much propriety and very real conformity with fact in the employment of this word by those who wish to describe what is done in schools. It is true that they very seldom expressly use the comparison which we have proposed of a school to a race-course; but they have no objection to the curriculum standing for the subjects which are taught and learnt in schools, and even for the methods by which they are taught. Just as horses are trained to run, to jump over fences and over water, so boys and girls are taught, in dealing with various subjects, to go through certain exercises and performances.

And there is this above all which gives the analogy a very strong claim to acceptance. We distinguish between other kinds of horses by naming the different sorts of work which they will have to do; some are cart-horses, and some carriage-horses, and some saddle-horses; but all these are distinguished from racers. To be sure racers contribute to the stock from which these other, work-a-day horses are bred; but they form a class apart. We need not say that they are an aristocracy, but we shall make ourselves ridiculous if we confuse them with the rest. They are in the world of horses, but not of it. Now while boys and girls remain in schools or colleges it might well be supposed that they correspond with racers, specially trained for a special performance. They are carefully sequestered; they are kept as much as may be out of the world and its occupations; they are being practised in exercises, which appear to be and often are alien to the exercises of the world; and the world marks the distinction very clearly by saying that, when school or college days are over, then work shall begin. But some of these pupils and students become so good at their scholastic and academic performances and, it is felt both by themselves and by the world, so wholly unfit for the activities of the world, that both choice and necessity make them pursue these exercises still further; still faster do they learn to move along their sheltered and fenced courses, still more difficult hurdles do they get the skill to take, still wider water jumps do they attempt with success; but upon the high road they do not set their feet, a load they do not draw,—in a word, they do not work. And it is those who have not the aptitude for these advanced studies, happily and yet unhappily, the vast majority, who, when they have done their best at the curriculum, leave it and take their place and make their way upon the common road of men.

It is not surprising that not in our own day for the first time the world has raised protests against the curriculum of schools. The protests have often been misdirected because those who made them have been ignorant and misinformed. But there has always been this of substantial value in their complaints, whether or not they have been fully justified in particular instances. The world is right in claiming that the schools and colleges should train men and women who can play largely and variously the parts which fall to men and women in the world; and right in condemning academic training if the only result for

those who are successful in it is that they are merely
capable of undergoing more and more of that training
upon a training ground which is cut off from the rest
of the world; and right again if the only result for
those who fall a little or very much short of success
in it is that they have accumulated a store of knowledge which they are ready to consign to some lumber-
room of their minds until they can get rid of it by
forgetting it; or have learnt some accomplishments
which they will never need to practise again; the world
is right if, when school days or college days are past,
they have then to learn to work. Such protests and
complaints, though, as we have admitted, they are
often ill-directed, suggest a positive statement of the
function of schools and colleges which may not always
be made by the authors of the protests and complaints. They suggest the positive statement that
schools and colleges should quite certainly prepare
those who pass through them for their business in
life, and point to the belief, half-formed, perhaps, and
inarticulate, that, so far as they fail of this object, the
reason is that the curriculum is too narrow; that the
track along which the training has been conducted
is fenced off too sharply from the world, and that
the exercises which are so diligently and perhaps so
expensively cultivated, whatever they may be, afford
no preparatory practice for those other exercises,
for which the general, comprehensive name is work.

There is some justice in these opinions expressly
declared or silently entertained; yet there is injustice
also. The distinction drawn between what is and

what is not work is hard and corresponds very imperfectly with the truth. Preparation for life is a larger matter than preparation for work, if work means those activities which can be paid for in money, or in political or social consideration. Life includes the whole of our activities, those which have no market value not less than those which have such a value: life is more than activities unless we are willing to include under the title of activities not only what we do but what we are. It certainly includes play; it embraces the luxuries as well as the necessities of existence; indeed to live is to claim luxuries as necessities, though it is not to confuse work with play. The distinction is unfortunate in its results for those who insist upon it, for it strongly tends to perpetuate the very state of things which they deplore. It tends to encourage the young in the determination to have "a good time" while they can, knowing that presently "work" and a time not good must await them. And it has the further effect of persuading them, when they have entered upon their work, to compress it into as narrow limits as they can, so that there may be a margin left, as wide as they can make it, for pleasure or even for life, which they not unnaturally learn to alienate altogether from their work.

There is a further objection which must be made against those who find fault with our schools and colleges on the grounds which we have considered. They expect or appear to expect these institutions to give their pupils practice in those special activities which are peculiar to the special work which will be

theirs in later life. Some apologists for the schools
and colleges reply that it is their function not to do
this, but rather to develop the powers of their pupils
in such a way that whatever they may have to undertake when they leave their schools and colleges they
shall come to it alert, intelligent and strong; ready
to discover what they have to do and to make a
beginning; resolute to persevere in face of obstacles,
to adapt themselves to the conditions in which they
are or to remould these conditions to themselves,
never losing sight of the end which they desire to
attain; and with the wit to profit by the lessons of
failure and of success, by the criticisms of their neighbours, and, most important of all, by the criticisms
which they direct upon themselves. To this there is
an easy and indeed a forcible reply. It may justly be
said that, though the objects which have been named
ought certainly to be sought, they can be sought and
found only by those who will take the pains to pursue
them by doing certain things. Quickness of perception, perseverance, adaptability, readiness to learn and
the practice of self-criticism are all good; but they
are to be had, if they are had at all, by those who
will act in such a manner, and engage in such activities
as call these qualities, if not into existence, at any
rate into effective operation. And the critics of schools
and colleges are bold to maintain that the exercises
which are practised in these places do not lead to the
development of these qualities.

It is not necessary to agree with them, or at the
moment to disagree: it is enough to listen to what

they say and to let them say more. Already they
have made two statements, first, that the exercises
of schools and colleges are not of the same kind as
those which will confront their pupils in later life;
and, second, that these exercises, such as they are,
fail to reach the ends for the attainment of which it
is professed that they were designed. What they go
on either to say in plain terms or very clearly to
suggest is that, if in school other exercises were substituted for those which are now customary, the pupils
might be provided with knowledge which they could
use, and at any rate be prepared by practice for the
discharge of duties which will fall to them, and perhaps
even acquire the very qualities which the accepted
studies claim but fail to achieve. Let education, they
say, be practical.

At this point in the argument a third voice is heard.
It is that of a man who speaks in a tone of annoyance
and declares that it matters nothing what boys and
girls or young men and women are taught in their
schools and colleges provided they follow the right
methods and are subjected to the proper discipline.
The intervention is useful, because it brings the two
main antagonists to closer grips and helps them to
approach a reconciliation. The advocates of the
schools have maintained that the traditional subjects
as customarily taught have the effect of forming a
certain type of mind and character which they believe
to be good and which their opponents would themselves praise if they could come to believe that it
really was formed by these subjects and the methods

associated with them. They now take heart to say that these subjects have a value in themselves, that they are worth possessing. We have then two pairs of statements or claims:

A (1) that the traditional subjects and methods produce a valuable kind of mind and character;

(2) that these subjects are in themselves valuable;

B (1) that subjects and methods which the world of after-school uses ought to be also the subjects and methods of the school world;

(2) that these subjects and methods may be able to form just that sort of mind and character which both parties agree in calling good.

The representatives of both parties can now look each other frankly and squarely in the face and can smile.

To the claim *A* (1) that the traditional subjects and methods produce a valuable kind of mind and character, both parties must admit an objection: it is that the claim cannot be proved. To prove it one would have to show that for making the valuable kind of mind and character these agencies and no others have been employed; but it is clear that a thousand other agencies touch and influence the most carefully secluded and guarded pupils.

The statement *A* (2) that these subjects are in themselves valuable provokes a question. Valuable, it may be asked, to whom and for what purpose?

To statement *B* (1) again a question may be raised. It may be asked, since not all the subjects and methods of the world of after-school could possibly be crowded into school or college life, which of these are to be selected and on what grounds is the choice to be made?

To statement B (2) a sufficient reply could be made in words of welcome to a pious hope, the fulfilment of which cannot be guaranteed.

The disputants have now come much nearer to one another than they were; or rather they see at last that the differences which divide them are less great than they supposed. Both parties are pledged to the belief that to do certain things will enable those who have practised these things to do other things afterwards. Both parties are pledged to the further belief that certain kinds of knowledge are worth possessing. If we examine these common beliefs we may yet find some evidence of difference between the two parties. We need not be surprised if the same formula, the same dogma holds some varieties of meaning as it falls from different lips. The upholders of tradition, as we may for the moment call them, claim that the study and practice of the classics, of history or of mathematics enable those who have engaged in them to pass readily and usefully to the practice and study of affairs, of business, of the work of the world. And the opposing party declares that this is too much to believe, because the work of the world (except for those who trade in classics, in history or in mathematics) is quite different from those studies; and in support of their own position they maintain that the preliminary study and practice of some of the things which will have to be learnt and done in the world

will assist us to study and practise other things of
the same kind.

The last contention is very plausible and fair-
seeming; but it cannot bear a close scrutiny. "What,"
we have to ask, "is meant by the same kind?" The
work of the world is very various; are we to say that
the work of a stockbroker and that of a sanitary
engineer are of the same kind? Are the work of a
bookseller and the work of a marine store dealer of
the same kind? of a cotton-broker and a tram-driver
of the same kind? The kind must have a very wide
definition if it is to include the special labours of all
these different persons. Or can we anticipate with a
sure and certain expectation that this boy will take
up, when he leaves school or college, this and not that
occupation or calling, that another boy will take up
another, and are we to give to each a training and a
preparation in the elements of the business which he
will presently make his own? We cannot forecast the
future with this sort of confidence, and, if we could,
what are the "elements" of each of those and of a
thousand other professions? Are the elements of one
different from the elements of another? Is it seriously
proposed that there should be classes or schools
specially provided, equipped, and directed so as to
enable children who are "born" grocers to be nour-
ished and trained in grocery; those who are "born"
clerks to be fostered "clerically"? If some children
are born with silver spoons in their mouths, we may
well be content with those monsters; children are not
born with paper-bags and scales in their hands or

fountain pens and copying lead pencils behind their ears. Time's hard graving tools may trace upon men's foreheads signs by which we may know their avocations even better than by the legends painted over their shop-fronts, beaten in brass upon their door-plates, or stamped upon their letter paper; men may wear badges of office and ceremonial dress; nakedness and hope are the happy insignia of childhood. No language could be found too rich for describing the bare possibilities of infants.

And since no language in which that theme could be fully set forth would satisfy those who do not recognise that the theme needs no argument, we may fall back at once upon the use of a dilemma one horn of which we have already offered to accommodate our adversaries. If they do not welcome what we have offered, if they will not maintain that the elements of the special trades and professions are themselves special, then we must inquire whether they think that the elements are general and common. Is the elementary education to be the same for those who may diverge after awhile from each other, taking some this, some that and some another path? They will be disposed, we think, to prefer this alternative. And we are bound to trouble them once more, for we must ask what more precisely this education is to be, of what it is to be composed, and to what end directed. And there is but one answer; its end is to prepare the young for commerce, for conversation, for dealing with the world; it must consist of speech, it must enable them to use the in-

strument of communication, it must give them access
to those things of which they are the heirs in virtue
of their humanity. To the whole of their inheritance
we know that they can never succeed; but the right
of entry they have, and it is for us to supply them
with the keys, for them to use as their fortune, their
ability, and their taste may suffer or direct them.

The acceptance of this doctrine would go far
towards making for us a coherent and unified society
and an orderly system of education. It would break
down the unhappy and mischievous distinction which
now stands between "elementary" and "secondary"
schools. Boys and girls must learn to speak their own
language, clearly, pleasantly, reasonably; and in it
to deal with matters of general, indeed of universal,
concern. The greatest matters are also the simplest,
and those with which we are all as human beings
interested. An elementary education should develop
and train ability to speak, to listen, to read, to write,
to reckon. It cannot do more; but less it must not
do. Upon this foundation the structure of further
education can be raised; but not without it: for
further education consists in learning ever more
clearly and fully what these words mean, what is involved in these activities. We may learn a second and
a third language, and have got no more education for
our labour, unless each is for us a new form of human
speech, by which we make ourselves known to our
fellows and come to understand them, tuning our ears
to catch the voice and the meaning of men as they
spoke long ago, or of others set far from us not in

time, but in measured distances of land or sea: and
with this lesson learnt, we fit our own voices to carry
to our contemporaries and successors what we have
to say to them of ourselves, and of our world, both
enriched by the practice of communication.

We still think and act as if there were several
kinds of education—elementary, secondary, technical,
academic. There may indeed be many modes of education, but there can only be one kind; there may be
many stages, but only one foundation; there may be
many roads, but only one goal—the discovery and
realisation made by a man of himself and of the world
in which he lives, and the serene enjoyment of both.
It is not only schools which would profit by framing
their programme for this end. Universities might fill
a greater part in the national life, if they were beyond
doubt or question devoted wholly to the quest of an
abundant life, and not, even in part or in appearance,
to the very different quest of a multitude of accomplishments. "Research for research's sake" would
soon follow "Art for art's sake," first into disrepute
and then into oblivion. It would be accompanied by
"Research for ostentation's sake," and Research for
pay." This is no plea for a "general" education, in
which many things or all things are attempted and
nothing done with precision and perfection; it is a plea
for a recognition of the plain truth that scholars and
other men live in the same world, and that it as much
befits "scholars" to be men of the world, as men of
the world to be "scholarly" in the methods and ends
which they set themselves.

CHAPTER VIII

SCIENCE AND SCIENCES

As in simple households breakages are by a pleasant convention attributed to the cat, so in that larger household which we call the state losses and failures are often set down to the account of the teacher. The range of this custom gives the measure of the teacher's authority and influence. It is all his fault, we say, and we are surprised if he does not at once admit his guilt. We should be entitled to feel surprise if our charge against him were quite general; for it would be ingratitude in him not to accept with courtesy a compliment, however clumsily paid. We feign for him a contempt which we do not at our heart entertain, and the proof is that, when things go ill, when our neighbours in other countries outstrip us in the arts of peace, or baffle us in those of war, we turn upon him as in some way responsible—why should he not agree? Why should he not thankfully agree and confess the justice of our accusation? To saddle him with responsibility is to credit him with power—power ill-used, misdirected or wrapped in a napkin and buried perhaps, but power still. Surely contrition should be easy for him, blended as it must be with conscious pride. Instead of telling us that parents, too, and statesmen and persons of every class and order in the community must share with

him his duty—a commonplace already current upon
the lips of men when they are talking at ease, but
denied when definite matters of urgent importance
are in hand, he should rather, so we feel, expose
himself to our attack and cherish the shafts which
we hurl against him "'Me—me—in me convertite
tela,' for your weapons are the insignia of my office."

But the teacher does not thus address us, and we
may ask why he misses his opportunity. It is for a
simple reason. Our charges are, in appearance at any
rate, too specific. "It is all his fault," we say and
repeat; but we go on to say in what special respect he
has failed us. And here we may well be unfair both
to him and to ourselves—unfair to him in charging
him with a particular offence, of which he could,
if we would but listen to him, show his innocence
by a very pertinent reply; and unfair to ourselves
in giving too narrow, and often a quite improper,
name to our real grievance. We complain that he
does not give us what we want, implying that he
could if he would; but, when we state explicitly what
we believe we want, we are apt to misjudge, not only
him, but ourselves. And we may run the risk of
confusing him by the variety of our specific demands
or our definitely named complaints. Now one thing,
now another, we lament; and, if he hastens to meet
in order our sundry and ill-considered claims, we have
another damaging count—we complain that the curriculum is too crowded. "Who crowded it?" he may
with decent indignation cry—Not he, that long-
suffering man.

We shall get what we ask for; if we do not get what we want and what we like, it is because we have not accurately interpreted our need and given it the right name. If our system of education does not satisfy us, it is we who are to blame—we, the parents, the citizens, the ordinary people who control it, provide it, pay for it. We are eager for power, shy of responsibility; but they go together. It is natural for us to forget this in these days of Government departments and more potent local authorities. Like teachers, the persons who fill these places may be viewed in two aspects; they are our representatives and servants, appointed to do what we want; they are also our equals, of the same stuff as the rest of us. To say this is not to disparage them. Let us grant that they are great men, of a delicate sensibility to judge what will best fashion the tender grace of youth to the mature beauty of manhood and bring golden promises to the rich fulfilment of developed and balanced powers, students of the methods and ideals of the past, and quick to devise fit methods for the ideals of our own time—the nobler the part they play, the more certainly is it shown to be the part of servants. If they have a special, it is also a partial responsibility; the general, the whole responsibility is ours shared with them as fellow-citizens. What then do we want? And what is it that we ask for to-day?

One demand is very often made, and expressed, in the form of a complaint; we complain of the neglect of science. Is it true that we want "science," or more of it than we have? That would seem to be our meaning.

We are, in fact, uncomfortable and alarmed[1]; we expect, of couse, to "muddle through," we are confident that all will be well at last; but we have the troublesome conviction in our minds that we should have done better and gone faster with the War, if we had had more "science"; we suspect that it is because they have had science as their ally or their slave that the Germans, having outraged the Western world, still hold out, weakened, we know, but unconquered, we admit. Not long ago, and then too in resentment and fear of German progress, it was "technical instruction" that we called for—that and more of that, and to-day it is "science." The call for science is loudly raised and by many persons who might be at a loss for an answer if they were asked what precisely they meant. And those who might have told us have been singularly reluctant to provide us with an interpretation of the word, for the neglect of science has been bewailed most bitterly by "men of science." They, of course, know what science is. Is it not their property, their creation?

And we, common men and women, dimly or painfully aware that something is amiss with us and with the body politic, are ready, only too ready, to put a name upon our failings. "What have we omitted?" we ask, and we get in response "you have neglected science." "To be sure, we have neglected science," is our echo; "those teachers in schools and Universities have failed us again." We thank the men of science and promise to speak to the defaulters and

[1] Written in July 1916.

tell them what we think of them. Addressed, arraigned, what have they put forward in defence? At first, and not unnaturally, they take up a legal mode of argument, and remind us that, at our instance, they are teaching science already; that, at our command, every Secondary school in receipt of public grants provides instruction in science, whatever else it may omit from its programme of studies; that the Universities, old and new, have increased their scientific equipment, enlarged their laboratories, doubled their staff of science teachers, and that "Elementary Science" has long had its vogue in Elementary schools. Is it more "science" that we need, and still more? The realm of science has been widened, new provinces and departments have been revealed and presently marked out and given over to specialists; and yet we are not satisfied; are we to await the opening of a wider horizon, an ampler dawn, when more new provinces, more new departments, and specialists, yet unborn, will be given us? Are we to hasten that day?

To them that have there shall be given, all the more certainly and abundantly if they eagerly seek and insistently demand. We have science and it is very likely that we shall get more science and more sciences. Is this what we really want? And what after all is science? Two common answers to these questions may be quickly considered. We are familiar with lists of subjects dealt with in our Universities in their Faculties of Science and in schools in their modern or scientific departments. Let us not attempt to be philosophical, the practical man will admonish us; these subjects are sciences, the total of these and similar subjects is what by general consent is called Science. Or we may offer another answer. By science we mean such knowledge of the world's material forces as will enable us to control them and turn them to our service. Science is the name of knowledge of that kind; let us get more science, and we shall be able more and more completely to master these forces. Our use of what we have is shown in our ability to get more; money we use to get more money; property of whatever sort to acquire more property, and with all this the weapons with which to fight for what we desire and to defend it against aggressors. Science shows us how to use what we have; if we can get more science, we shall use what we have to greater advantage. Science provides us with the machinery for acquisition. We have machines to carry us and our goods by land and sea, to traffic and increase our store—machines for collecting and combining the materials of our food, our clothing, our dwellings; we have instruments and drugs for mitigating pain, and correcting human deformities and stimulating the tired energies of men; and we have—wrought with not less care and lavished upon a far vaster scale— the engines of destruction and of death. And all these we owe to science.

Is it pretended, the advocates of science so conceived ask, that classical scholarship will issue in these glorious results? Will history and music achieve these ends? And there is only one reply. These studies do not yield these fruits. Classical scholarship breeds its kind—more classical scholarship; history and music, pursued, lead to more music and a more elaborate history. And the persons who are devoted to these matters do not extend our domain over nature or strengthen our mastery of her powers. Let us then have fresh recourse to science; for, it is said, we have neglected her, and we suffer for our failure. Much we have profited by scientific work done; much more may we hope to profit by renewed application: and to enforce a moral on ourselves we raise the German spectre.

Now the men of science who in this country have lately been upbraiding us for neglecting science have not said that they are themselves less eminent than men of science in Germany or elsewhere—they would probably be guilty of a false and mischievous modesty if they did; they have not even told us that there is less "science" here than there. But what appears is that science and scientists are less sought out here than elsewhere for their advice and their help. No doubt more and more our great manufacturers employ scientific men; but still not enough. They should take to such men problems of which they see the importance but not the solution, and employ them for their purposes. Scientific men are not all unwilling, we may conceive, to be employed and paid; we need business men of enough imagination to turn them to account. The sterility of learned persons is notorious; the useful energy of business men is a theme not unsung; but if the busy bees refused to visit the flowers, seeking honey and carrying the fertilising pollen upon their industrious thighs, flowers of the field might be as unproductive as scientists wilting upon their lonely stalks.

But scientists, however exactly similar in other respects, differ from flowers in having voices. They should use them; but they should select the proper audience. They have something to sell; let them call out to those who are able to buy, not without money or without price. The rich manufacturers, the capitalists should be their prey or their beneficiaries. To them they should turn and say: "You have great wealth; you control machinery; we can improve your machinery, of whatever kind it may be; we can make it more productive; it shall move at a greater speed than any yet attained; and, again, the by-products of your processes we can turn to better and better purpose, if you will listen to us; and things of which you have only dreamed, or things yet undreamed of, we can put into your possession." They are too reticent and too retiring; they have allowed themselves the coyness of Celia; they must practise the "coming on disposition" of Rosalind, and persuade the rich to employ them. The number of men in England who would spend a thousand pounds if they were convinced that they would get back two thousand must still be considerable; the men of science might find that it was very large and even overwhelming; it might turn out that the demand for men of science would be so insistent and so general that more men of science would be needed, and then, as they cannot be manufactured, they must be reared. Schools and Universities, hitherto the dusty treasuries of unmarketable things, would be caught by the breath of the new movement; they would become the training ground for young scientists, students with a career before them, being prepared to supply the world with what it wanted. Then ancient studies would be abandoned, if they could not be remodelled; many of their teachers would be dismissed, perhaps with pensions large enough to remind them of the uses of money, or consigned to more appropriate asylums. Others might be collected by the curious, like Pekingese terriers for their fluffy prettiness, or like love-birds for their touching amiability, for their affectionate little ways. And science harnessed to industry and commerce would produce more and more wonderful machines, the means of communication would be made more rapid throughout the World, and—there would not be an idea to be shared by men who had enslaved themselves and lost their souls.

If all this is a travesty of what men of science desire it is a travesty which not a few of their supporters will, if they are not prevented, be disposed to force upon them and upon us all. For it is too little perceived even now that it is not in virtue of science or knowledge of sciences, or the application of them to this or that special object, that the Germans have grown strong. They have grown strong because they have set certain ends clearly before them, and have sought for the means by which these ends could be achieved. But, what is far more important, their ends have been organised, co-ordinated, unified. They have known more exactly and clearly than we have known what they wanted from science, and they have seen to it that there should be a supply of men prepared by their *general* as well as by their special training to supply what was asked of them, viz., their contribution to a system of ends, to a conception of their state. That system, that conception, we have come to hate, for, while it excludes much that we think essential, it includes much that we think hostile to humanity. It is a system which sooner or later humanity will break; but it is strong, not because it is good, but because it is a system, and, more than that, because it is a body of belief. And it will be broken by humanity because its violent challenge has made or is making humanity seek a system, a body of belief, and suffers it no longer to be contented with vague, indefinite, unconcerted, disorganised fragments of belief. The strength of German education as of German civilisation, has been its centralisation, in its organisation. Organisation sounds ill in English ears, and hasty critics warn us in education, as they are pleased to regard it, to be on our guard against organisation. For they make two mistakes about organisation; first, they think of it as the rigid arrangement in separate departments, of special interests and concerns, each one complete in itself and independent; whereas, if it is to be real, it must mean not less than the co-ordination of all these departments within and as parts of a whole; and then, they think of it in the terms of material things, and of office routine, and express themselves in the language of Committees.

But organisation means the embodiment of a creed, unifying a community by expressing the common meaning of its members.

Now it is easier to make a mean than a majestic creed; it is easier to win adherence and allegiance (for a time) to the narrow interpretation of the needs and desires of a society or a party (needs which become themselves at once the narrower and the more compact for such an interpretation), than to secure loyalty to ideas which have not yet established amongst themselves a vivid relationship, expressed in a form at once clear and elastic. And this is the reason why Germany has been so powerful: she has known her own mind; she has been mistress of her own resources, she has ordered them to a clearly seen end. And organisation for her has meant more than mere officialism, for her officialism has been symbolic. It has represented the focussing, in all departments of her life, of her varied energies upon the maintenance and enlargement of that life.

We have indeed had, and now more passionately than ever cherish, ideals, many of which Germany has either never known, or forsworn; but we have not had organisation in its proper sense, we have not had co-ordinating organisation, the comprehensive expression a belief in which our ideals are harmonised and wrought both severally and collectively to their highest power. This has been our misfortune and our fault. It is nowhere more fully illustrated than in our speech and action in regard to education. For we have not yet regarded Education as a part of the

national life, inseparable from other parts, affecting
them and influenced by them; and within the wide
and loosely determined province which we call Education we have not yet achieved and scarcely attempted
organisation. We have not made our way to a vitalising and unifying conception of it as a whole. We
began, forty years after we were warned, to organise
our Secondary schools; but we can hardly imagine
that Matthew Arnold would have been pleased with
what we have done in his name. We have set up a
new class of schools, but we have not illumined our
national education as a whole with a new and radiant
idea. And the result is that, for all the good these
new Secondary schools have done as yet in detail (and
in detail they have done much good), our national
education is not more, but less, systematised than it
was before. We have not yet decided how and when
pupils are to get into these new schools, nor how and
when they are to get out of them, nor yet what to do
while they remain in them. But a society is a system
of living relationships; and to throw into a society,
already ill-organised, a society which not quite perfectly deserves that title, a new and unrelated element,
is not to help it towards its proper goal, but to hinder
its progress. We may justly entertain the highest
hopes for our new Secondary schools; but if they are
to fulfil these hopes we must form a clear conception
of the service which they are to render to our national
life in general, and of the relation in which they are
to stand to our Elementary schools, to our Public
schools, and to our Universities.

It may quite truly be said that the study of nature and her forces is necessary for the education of the human mind together with a study of man and his powers and achievements: it may well be granted that some study of nature and her forces, of the subjects called collectively science, is necessary for an intelligent and fruitful study of the humanities: it should surely be granted that some command of language is necessary for formulating scientific problems, for expressing the solutions which we may reach and not less for understanding what problems and what answers have already risen in the minds of our own people and of workers in other countries. It is not hard in general terms to harmonise these two claims; it should not be impossible even in practice to make some useful combination of them. "Arts" students in our Universities might quite well, without loss to their literary, historical or other studies, be required, all of them (as those who are being prepared for teaching in Elementary schools have been required) to give some part of their time to some scientific subject; and "Science" students not less well might be required to give some of their time to literature or history. But this, though it would help us forward, is not enough; for even with this safeguard the danger, which we have not hitherto escaped, would still threaten and even overtake us. For it is not knowledge of any or of all these things that we chiefly need: and the danger is lest persons who have acquired some or even much knowledge in these matters may think they have done all that they ought

to do. The danger is lest we should cut off both
literature and science from their roots.

No more "practical" utterance upon our present
problem could well be found than a sentence of Professor Burnet's in his *Greek Philosophy from Thales to
Plato.* "We find," he says, "that every serious attempt
to grapple with the problem of reality brings with it
a great advance in positive science, and that this has
always ceased to flourish when interest in that problem was weak[1]." Technology needs no advocates;
their name is legion; but, though technology depends
on science, the application of science to the comfort
and the discomfort of men must be clearly distinguished from science itself. We may make ourselves
more comfortable in peace, and our enemies more
miserable in war, by increased application of scientific
knowledge to these ends; but if these are the ends we
set out to seek we may soon kill science itself. And
we have to remember that science is already threatened by the very progress of the sciences. I shall
quote a philosopher once more: "The world of
thought," wrote Professor Hobhouse in his *Theory
of Knowledge*, "at the present day is in a somewhat
anomalous condition. We have come to the point
where science seems to stand in real danger of being
ruined by her own success. The mass of accumulated
fact in which she justly prides herself has become too
vast for any single mind to master.... Year by year it
becomes more difficult to take any sort of view of the
whole field of knowledge, which should be at once

[1] pp. 11, 12.

comprehensive and accurate. It results that positive knowledge can scarcely be said any longer to have a general purpose or tendency. Intellectually it is an age of detail[1]."

But, where there is no purpose or tendency, organisation has either failed or ceased to exist. An age of detail is an age without belief, and belief is the vitalising source and main-spring of organisation. Professor Hobhouse wrote the passage just quoted twenty years ago. On the same page he adds: "So far from seeing our way to a near or distant synthesis, we are more disturbed than ever when we turn from science to philosophy. Instead of uniting the sciences, philosophy threatens to become a separate and even a hostile doctrine." And on the next page he proceeds: "An elegant scepticism about science takes the place of the elegant scepticism of theology with which our fore-fathers were familiar." But, dismissing scepticism "as a mere symptom of temporary intellectual paralysis," he is not without good hope of a synthesis yet to be achieved, and few writers are better entitled to the hope, for few have done more to bring it to fulfilment. If it is easier for a camel to pass through the eye of a needle than for a rich man to enter into the Kingdom of heaven, the reason is that the camel after all is one camel, and the "rich" man, playing many different rôles, being many persons, may not win that oneness which we call personality. There is so *much* of him that at last there have come to be *many* of him. But that is just what has befallen education;

[1] Preface, p. vii.

there is so much of it, that there have come to be *many* of it; so much knowledge that, in the name of convenience, we have set up many knowledges. We have named them, labelled them, departmentalised them, and taken the soul out of them. Of course, we must learn science, and the sciences; of course we must apply them to practical uses. But why? not in order that we may get more armchairs and more explosives; but in order that we may get at reality and discover and possess ourselves in a life which, if rich, shall yet be intelligent because unified, and in a society which, if large and made of many elements, shall yet be governed by a unifying belief. To this end the development of scientific studies must contribute an essential service; if the vision of this end does not inspire us, the progress of science will but yield the increase of detail, and its success will be its disaster and our undoing.

CHAPTER IX

WORK AND PLAY

THE belief which the preceding pages have been written to justify is that a man's education is the long process by which he learns to subordinate himself to the control of an ideal society. This society is to give him the highest development of his powers such as they may be, by co-ordinating them with the kindred but not identical powers of his fellows, trained, like himself, by the necessity of co-operation, to such perfection as is appropriate to them. Perfect adjustment is the only perfect freedom, but freedom is formed in service of dominant ideal. But service in an ideal society cannot be rendered by slaves or automata. That society, which moulds its members to its own eternal design, is itself formed and brought into being by them; created, they are also creators, working slowly through an intelligent recognition of the claims of any temporal and visible society in which they find their place. Here too, and here already, they are servants but by the very perfection of their service they refashion the city, the state, in which they dwell to the pattern of that other city in which they claim membership. Service, subjection, subordination, are words and notions distasteful to many people. The advocates of freedom unfettered, the apostles of individuality find ready listeners and enthusiastic followers.

Few men have done so much to ennoble our conception of Education as Professor T. P. Nunn; to few is the present writer so much indebted for generous help, for stimulating advice; to few indeed, would he more gladly offer if he might a tribute of affectionate and respectful admiration. There will, then, be little risk of misunderstanding if use is made here of a brilliant section of a very remarkable work[1], written by a colleague and a friend, for bringing into clearer relief the central doctrine, of this, so very different, book.

Professor Nunn tells us that his "purpose is to reassert the claim of Individuality to be regarded as the supreme educational end, and to protect that ideal against both the misprision of its critics and the incautious advocacy of some of its friends." We have urged, on the other side, that though individuality may be *an* educational end, it is an end which can only be attained by those who seek another and a larger end. "Individuality," to be sure, is a hard word, yet it is employed in a more intelligible and more consistent sense in this work than in many others, and there can be no doubt that the author has deserved and won much approval. His argument, strong and flexible, is always urged with manifest sincerity of conviction, and often with a judicious caution. In the passage already quoted, if it is maintained that some critics misprise the ideal of individuality, it is allowed that some of its friends are

[1] T. P. Nunn, *Education, its Data and First Principles*. (Arnold, 1920.)

incautious. The "misprision" is due, perhaps, in part to the doubt in which readers are involved as to what the claim for Individuality really means: the very fairness with which in this work it is for the most part upheld makes them wonder whether everything that they would set over against that claim is not generously granted. Yet for plain persons the word suggests that when we set up a claim for Individuality, you and I and any other man desires each one of us to "be himself," to "go his own way," and if he is to make a contribution to the general welfare of society to make such contribution as he himself thinks fit, and to make it as he chooses. This sense of the word, seems to be adopted in the chapters entitled "Play" and "The Play-Way in Education." In these chapters much, if not all, the reserve which marks other parts of the work is abandoned; we shall therefore consider them, in the hope either of revealing the grounds of disagreement or of establishing the terms of a reconciliation. The importance which their author gives to the conception of Play, and for the purpose of this argument, to his interpretation of it may be learnt from his own words: "it is hardly extravagant to say that in the understanding of play lies the key to most of the practical problems of education."

The spirit of play, we are informed, is intangible and elusive. It is also very generous, for, though the alert and unwearying writer tries hard in the course of nearly forty pages to put his hand on it, it escapes him for all his ingenuity; and with a smile, if not with laughter to be heard by mortal ears, proves that he is right. Intangible and elusive, yet play is known well enough by common folk, who, agreeing, "that it is impossible to maintain a psychological antithesis between play and work[1]," are satisfied that there is an ethical, a practical difference between the two.

"An agent," Dr Nunn says, "thinks of his activity as play if he can take it up or lay it down at choice or vary at will the conditions of its exercise; he thinks of it as work if it is imposed on him by unavoidable necessity, or if he is held to it by a sense of duty or vocation." This is "the basis of the limited validity which we grant to the antithesis between play and work." Dr Nunn says that we can readily understand the difference by analysing any activity, "for example, eating one's dinner." We must eat; here is necessity; but is a man at work when he is eating his dinner? Not in the language of the vulgar. But, even if eating dinner is "work," it must be granted that some people, "a fortunate minority of us," have freedom, not indeed complete but "considerable," in choosing what we shall eat and how and where we shall eat it; and with this freedom we may presumably either change the "work" of eating into play or at least pleasantly and decently disguise it.

We cannot, to be sure, often eat foods and drink liquors for which we cannot pay, or more than once take poisons; yet if our freedom is thus sadly limited we may make the best of what we have. We may, an occasion, go out to a fashionable restaurant, and,

[1] Bradley, "On Floating Ideas and the Imaginary," *Mind*, N.S. No. 60; cited by Nunn *ob. cit.* p. 76.

if the occasion were appropriate, our expedition and
our meal might justly be called a play; but if we elect
"a chop at home," much as we may ordinarily prefer
that to the most splendid banquet, can we be said
to "play" as we eat that nourishing and now, alas!
too rare food? No! We do not play with a mutton
chop—we eat it, devour it, wolf it; we cannot play
with it. Is it to be said that we "toy" with a mutton
chop? The word is unfamiliar in this use; but, if we
even so employed it, we should mean that we did not
eat the chop, owning ourselves unequal to its potency
or insensitive to its rich appeal. But why might the
restaurant dinner be play? The reason is plain: because we might go to it "for fun"? Why could not the
"chop at home" be play? Because we cannot eat a
chop "for fun"; the feat is not recorded of men. The
constraint under which we eat is, we are told, external
and ultimate. Ultimate, perhaps; but is it external?
We are not apt to regard ourselves, as the victims of
"forcible feeding," when we eat because we are
hungry. The illustration is distressing: let us very
quickly abandon it. And the text is the main thing,
the positive, though guarded statement, that there is
a "limited validity" in the "antithesis between play
and work."

The difference may be put thus: We say "I must,"
when we are talking about work; we say "I need not,
but I will," when we are talking about play. But
Dr Nunn is eager to bring the spirit of play into all
that we do. He has very clearly and forcibly used an
argument which is frequently attempted by less

adroit writers, and by thinkers who lack his courage and his perception. Not the least of the merits of this book is the orderly contribution made by each part to the main thesis, and the chapters which deal with play are subservient to the general argument. But we are disposed to think that the accomplished and learned author might have come nearer to the truth if in treating play he had taken the risk of being inconsistent with his general theory, and that if he had taken the risk he would have abandoned the theory itself. For we are not ready to accept Individuality as the "supreme educational end," or to suppose that the end can be stated in any simple word or formula. The end when justly stated must also be illogically stated; it must be as various and as intolerant of a strict definition as life itself. To seek individuality is good, but to lose it is good; to yield to society and to defy society are both proper tasks for men, who must be in the world and yet not of it; who must be themselves, but can only discover themselves by finding other selves than their own; who must die in order to live. It is granted, indeed, that the individual must make his contribution to the general welfare of the Society, the world, in which he lives; but the admission is followed by the claim that he must be free to make it as he chooses, in the form which he elects; and this is a freedom which the world cannot grant, because it would be a freedom without meaning.

There is no gainsaying the statement that play is important; but when we ask what play is our counsellors are prone to fail us. They speak of its characteristics; or they look with eyes not undimmed by kindly tears upon the activities of early childhood and declare that these are plays and are prompted and inspired by the spirit of play. What are these characteristics? One is said to be spontaneity; another is joy. What we do of our own accord and with delight is play. Or, again, if in any activity we seek nothing else, nothing beyond and outside the activity itself, then, it is said, we are at play. And once more we are told that if, though there be an end proposed, that end is a "make-believe" and different from the "real" ends of ordinary life, then the activity in which we seek this pretended end is play. Now we may recognise these characteristics, and may even hasten to say that they are characteristics of play; but we are not satisfied that they are the *differentiae* of play: indeed, quite clearly and beyond dispute, these are the characteristics of some activities which we also call "work." Or is it to be believed that we never work "spontaneously," never "with joy"; that no work is ever an end in itself; that in work we never set before ourselves a "make-believe" or pretended end? What advance or discovery has ever been made except by men who framed and tested a hypothesis which was untrue to the world of fact and science as at that moment accepted? Was the hypothesis justified? Then the "real" world was real no longer; old things were passed away and behold all things were new. The very passion with which many good people now bid us bring the spirit of play into work

proves them to be almost on our side. They long
to make work one with play; we reply that, that
though work is not play, the characteristics which
they find in play have always been present in all work
which is not bondsmen's work; but we hold that play
has other notes which they have not remarked, and
work qualities different from those of play in addition
to those which it shares with play.

The apologists of play admit and even proclaim
that play is not work, and we must try to find out
what is the difference between them. We are not
much helped by the very instructive observations
which they make about the function of play, its use
for us. It may well be true that the performance of
certain activities, common in the infancy and childhood of other animals and of human creatures, gives
admirable and necessary practice for repeating these
activities or some of them in later, mature, life. In
infancy, or childhood, it is argued, young creatures
make experiments upon themselves and upon the
world, upon their own varied and growing powers
and upon the answering and resistant or encouraging
forces of the world; they train themselves to agility,
to speed, to endurance. They mimic the serious occupations of their parents, they recall in strange antics
the feats of distant ancestors, perhaps they hit upon
untried and certainly exhibit unrecorded modes of
exercise. The puppy pursues his innocent and un-
docked tail; the boy throws and catches a ball, he
fights little battles that tax his strength, he hunts, he
builds; his sister is his playmate and his rival, and

his despair; she too has her occupations, she nurses her doll, she minds her fancy-built home. The boy is preparing himself, all unconsciously, for manhood; the girl, for womanhood. All this is a beautiful and engaging spectacle for philosophic middle-age. Professor Nunn tells us that we have here a "biological device," he speaks of Nature as a person, and because Nature (like play) is elusive he must call nature "she": she has devices, the "devices" of play for building up the young, fashioning them for what will presently befall, getting them ready for the burden of life. It is a theme for poets, and indeed they have made it very much their own, and given it back to the plain prosaic world embellished by their art.

But we have two questions to ask—Are *all* the activities of infancy and childhood play? Or are we to say that some are play and others not? There is eating, for example. In eating, we conceive, children and other young creatures are preparing themselves for the stress and strain of after years. Is eating play? It is surely as natural and necessary as hunting, fighting, building, doll-nursing. And sleep? Is this play? Probably no one will be found to claim eating, drinking, and sleeping as part of the play of children and other young creatures. These things, it will be said, they must do: they cannot help themselves. Is play, then, the general name for their waking activities other than eating and drinking? But it may quite well be said, and indeed has been stated on high authority, that a boy can no more help running after a ball or pursuing another boy than a kitten can help pouncing upon a reel of cotton drawn before it. Is a chicken then at play when it pecks on the ground for seed? No, it is replied, the chicken is not at play, because already it is independent of its parents; it is earning its living, it is depending on its own efforts for a livelihood. How low down in the animal scale may we go and still find play? Here is an interesting question the answer to which might help us to discover the meaning of play, but we cannot directly pursue this problem.

The distinction between the "work" of the chicken and the "play" of the kitten, the puppy or the child is drawn by those who make use of it to help their argument that play is free, a proof and exhibition of spontaneity. But if those creatures cannot help "playing," where is the freedom, where the spontaneity? We have used these two words "freedom" and "spontaneity" as if they were equivalent, and so indeed they are often used to the darkening of counsel. A spontaneous action may perhaps be described as one which results from the loosening of some spring within the creature that does the action, though even so we are left to guess what it is that releases the spring and why. But a free action is something much more important than this, something, at any rate, very different. A free action is an action selected from alternatives. Accordingly, if a boy cannot help himself from adopting this or that mode of play, whichever it is that he adopts, he is not free. To this question we shall presently come back.

It is worth while at this point to observe that the
freedom which is postulated for children (and other
creatures) in their play has very narrow limits; the
conditions in which play is conducted are indeed so
clear, so stringent, and (quite apart from those which
are drawn by the native abilities or disabilities of the
player) drawn so firmly by forces not his own, traced
we may say by a will not his own, that, though we
may like to keep the word, we are constrained to
admit that this freedom is a very little thing. The
epigram, quoted with approval warmer than it deserves, that we are young so long as we play rather
than we play so long as we are young, serves our
purpose. For what is this youthfulness? It is a state
in which we depend for maintenance and protection
upon other people. Now there are no names for
constraint more apt that these names; there is no
constraint more rigid than that which is enforced by
maintenance and protection. No doubt, while maintenance and protection are afforded to it, the young
creature may accumulate a store of superfluous energy,
but this energy is superfluous for self-maintenance
and self-protection because maintenance and protection are provided from without. And if one of the
principal purposes sought or ends achieved by this
external maintenance and protection is the safe-
guarding of the energy of the young creature against
its own extravagance and folly, another principal end
is the safe-guarding of the elder generation, the
society into which the new comer is arrived, from the
depredation, the extravagant misuse to which the

young will, unless they are severely limited, subject their elders.

And we cannot forget that the freedom of any young creature is closely hedged about by the liberties of other young creatures, who may even defy and incontinently transgress the boundaries of their own making or made by others which confront them.

If play has the characteristics which its modern advocates so painfully claim for it, then it is clear that infancy and early childhood are periods in which we did not play. For there is no play except in con-tradistinction to work . To say this is not to disparage either work or play or to maintain that we must choose between them, cleaving to the one and aban-doning the other; we must take both, one at a time, for the ordinary dull days when we are at that low level which we call our average height, but both to-gether when we rise, as sometimes we all rise, to a serener altitude. But there is a period apparently when the distinction, the difference between work and play has not yet been apprehended, and it would seem to be clear that until the distinction is appre-hended work and play do not yet exist—in other words, the activities in which we engage do not yet deserve either the name of work or the name of play.

CHAPTER X

ORIGINALITY AND CONVENTION

SOME support for the conclusion which we have now reached may be got from Professor Drever[1]. He tells us that the "work tendency" begins to show itself at about the age of seven. A contrast, in fact begins to make itself felt between what must be and what may be. The moment at which this discovery is made is a critical moment. It involves an analysis of the simple, single, world of infancy into two parts, which seem to break away from one another so completely as to become two worlds, sometimes remote one from the other, and yet sometimes menacingly near. And with the violent shock of a world breaking in twain comes the more cruel because more intimate discovery that the happy and hitherto thoughtless, inhabitant of a single and pleasant universe is himself divided by the sharp edge of thought which has cut his world in two. The main business of the rest of life consists in solving the problem which is thus created. If the problem is regarded merely as a paper puzzle it may be said that three possibilities offer themselves for trial. Either we must live in the world of work, or we must live in the world of play, or we must reconcile two worlds, parts of a broken world, and bring them into a fresh unity. But the problem is not a paper puzzle for the exercise of a logical

[1] *Instinct in Man*, p. 229.

ingenuity; it is a practical problem, and in fact we know that there is only one solution, namely, the last, that of reuniting and so reinterpreting the sundered parts of the primitive or childish universe.

Some fanatics make the attempt to live for play, just as other fanatics not less dangerous to themselves and to their neighbours make the attempt to live for work. Fanatics of both sorts seek to sunder and keep separate partners whom God has joined, and whose union, depending as all vital unions do upon difference, has been apparently shattered by the thought which has discovered this difference. Upon those who will play and do nothing but play, the notion, the idea of work breaks, the idea of necessity, of compulsion, of right; upon these who will work and do nothing but work, the notion of play, the idea of it, sheds a rare but disconcerting ray, with the effect of penetrating their hearts with the shaft of discontent. Much as they may have won by their zeal for play or for work, they have ruined, these partisans, the one thing needful, and that is the reconstructed unity of themselves and of their world. We have used the words "reconstructed unity," and they may have served our purpose decently well; yet it is necessary to remember that the unity, the wholeness, which is "reconstructed" is not the same as the unity which has been dissolved by thought, by appreciation, by conscious enquiry. Rather it should be said that unity is at once created and threatened by the analysis which discovers divers elements in what was an undiscriminated, undifferentiated whole. Infancy has a wholeness for us older persons to admire or to deplore; but there is no wholeness for an eye which cannot perceive it. And when the eye learns to perceive unity, the moment is come for it to discover variety, discrepancy, contrariety, the elements of strife as well as the elements of concord.

So an untrained ear may catch and delight to hold a sound which gives it an unintelligent pleasure; but a trained ear hears not a sound, but a harmony of concerted sounds, and perceives the whole which they compose because it appreciates the several different sounds of which that total consists. It is then legitimate to say that the trained ear creates the harmony which it perceives, and that for the untrained ear the unity which, in default of better and more exact language, we said that it apprehended did not really exist.

The passage in Professor Drever's book to which reference has already been made calls for further notice. When he speaks of the work tendency he contrasts it with the tendency towards experimentation. Experimentation is in his view one of the elements of play—when we experiment we make trial in this way or that of the world to see what will happen; when we work we act upon the world expecting a result for our action. "The interest in experimentation is satisfied with whatever result emerges, while in the case of 'work' the result which emerges is not satisfactory unless it is the result aimed at, or sufficiently approximating to that to be taken for it by the child. Though the 'work' tendency may therefore be distinguished from instinctive experimentation it may also be regarded as a development from it. And experimentation certainly co-operates in rendering results, of little significance in themselves, sufficiently interesting as results and as the results intended to stimulate long and strenuous effort."

Aristotle tells us that a child cannot be truly happy. The conditions of true happiness a child cannot master, its elements he cannot grasp and keep together. It may be said not less justly that a child cannot truly play, until he has discovered the meaning of work and conceived a desire for it. To see what will happen is a pleasure which cannot be enjoyed by a person who cannot distinguish between happening and the result of intention, the effect of considered and purposive action. The epigram "we are young as long as we play" is misleading: it would be better to say that we cannot begin to play until we have learned to work. The earliest distinction between work and play—a distinction like others which, as we shall have to note, must be caught up into a harmony or unity—is then the distinction between "must" and "may." "I must do this because I must achieve that" is what we say to ourselves about work. "I may do, I have leisure for doing, I can afford to do that and risk the consequences or pay the bill" is what we say to ourselves about play. And we say neither of these things to ourselves during that period, long or short, in which childhood is quite erroneously said to disport itself. There would indeed be some excuse for those who should pretend that that period of childhood is a period of unbroken work. No one can have failed to remark the apparent seriousness with which young children "play." They "play" with their fingers and their toes with a solemnity with which great statesman may handle the destinies of empires or with which aldermen eat their dinners. But they are not really "playing" at all; they are engaged in a process as vitally important as that of eating and drinking. A healthy infant takes his milk with a look of absorption which would suggest that the whole world were offering him a teat and that his life depended on sucking it dry. His look does not belie the fact, and yet the plain and magnificent fact may elude us who, having left the happy confines of terrestrial infancy, have yet not made our way, infants a second time, into the kingdom of Heaven. The fact is indeed simple enough, but, since infancy has no title, and pretends none, to speech, speech cannot describe it, without formal contradiction. The infant, then, who absorbs the world, his world, has no name for it and does not distinguish it from himself. To begin with, the world, his world, is a composite whole, himself and his mother's breast; but he has neither desire nor power to analyse this total. Already he has other needs than the need of food, but even these he cannot at first distinguish. The "world" which is his nourishment is also his warmth, his support, his waking, his sleeping, his everything: in a word, it is himself.

But presently that world exhibits itself to him by withdrawing itself for a space, for a time, and he discovers it by its comparative absence, by its remoteness. Then he discovers himself, and the discovery is a series of discoveries. Food, warmth, support, waking, sleeping, all these things which were, all together, himself (things which we, looking at him from without, were ready to call himself *and* his world, distinguishing between them) now present themselves in succession; he is cold and wants—warmth; he is falling and wants—support; he wakes and wants—company; he sleeps and wants—the enfolding arm. He is not suffered to want long; but he must be suffered to want long enough; there must be an interval, a pause, a vacancy; in that interval he has the leisure and the necessity to find himself; that vacancy he fills with himself. But the self which he fashions, he fashions from materials, of which he now becomes conscious; he is a creature, who hungers, who thinks, who craves so many several things. The world stands over against him; it is the source, the varied and fruitful source from which he may satisfy these varied and exigent needs. Again our grown-up language leads us astray. We said the child "discovers himself." At the moment, a few lines higher, that was legitimate; but now we must rather say that he discovers several selves, a hungering self, a thirsting self, and others. And who is it that makes that discovery; who is he? The hungering self, with which he is, or to us and to himself seems to be identified, ceases to urge its claim when hunger is satisfied, and with its claim withdraws (I do not say cancels or annihilates) itself; the thirsting self appears and, when thirst is quenched, retreats; the other selves present and call away themselves. And *he* remains; but himself he does not see; of himself he very slowly becomes aware; and he becomes aware of himself as we, older people, become aware of silence when voices are hushed, or of darkness, when light is quenched, or of sound when silence is cleft to its core, or of light when darkness is gathered up, as a veil, with invisible hands.

That permanent remainder that eternal opposite, that background upon which rival selves show themselves, and which while they hold the stage they blot out—that is he. "Blot out," I said; it is an ink-stained word. For the child, the permanent self is not blotted out by the recurrent selves; it is dazzled out by them, it is out-coloured by them, while they exercise their brief and bright dominion; and they recur so soon, and they interchange so quickly, that the intervals between the scenes and acts are very little noticed, or, if they are prolonged, sleep drops like a curtain not upon the spectacle, but upon the spectator's soul. Yet intervals there are, how rare and brief soever; and sleep's curtain falls sometimes too slowly, and the spectator looking to see the performing selves sees his own eyes reflected from a world empty but for them. It is a vision he cannot yet endure; and he buries his head in his mother's breast, he grasps his father's hand; soon the curtain drops and sleep shuts the senses up, or half-releases them to act upon the twilit stage of dreams, phantom shadow dreams to the drowsing self. "I dreamed," the child announces when he wakes; or "You were dreaming" his mother tells him "I" "You"; the problem remains. Who is this spectator?

Once again, we must attempt to make the language which we have used more accurate, and to do this we must enquire more closely into the conditions in which it may be properly used. The truth is that the child never becomes the spectator of his selves (the hungering, thirsting, laughing, crying, selves) until he has had that experience which we tried just now to describe, the experience of seeing, if but for a moment, his self. The result of that vision is to make him more than a spectator: it makes him a critic, a judge. Henceforth he learns to arrange his selves in an order of importance and preference; he learns at the same time to relate his several selves to the world or the worlds in which he lives. And the main results of his study are that he finds that some of his selves are more valuable and necessary to himself than others, which may, however, be on occasion more attractive; he finds, further, that some of his selves are more valuable and necessary than the rest to the people with whom he has to live; that some of his selves may be very pleasant to these people, but pleasant upon some occasions and not on all; that some again of his selves are unpleasant to these people, who show their disapproval with marked and increasing severity; and that yet others are tolerated, because neither pleasant nor unpleasant, but indifferent.

He learns a scale or scales of values. To begin with,

his estimates are hard and inelastic; he contrasts too
sharply what is necessary with what is pleasant,
failing to remark the pleasantness of much that is
necessary, and the necessary character of much that
is pleasant. He contrasts too sharply what is pleasant
to himself with what is pleasant to other people, or
what is applauded by them or merely suffered by
them, or what they will on no condition permit. He
makes a hundred mistakes; there is no rule to guide
him unerringly; but in the main he is right; he learns
that for his own sake and for his neighbours some
things must be, other things may be, and others
again must not and may not. In learning to make
these estimates of value, it is evident that he is also
learning to make estimates of occasions also. There
is a time for this, and another time for that, and no
time at all for something else. He finds once more,
that the occasions for some of the things he has to do
(*i.e.* for the manifestations of some of his selves) are
frequent or prolonged or both; and that the occasions
for other things that he is disposed to do are rare or
short or both. And he may too readily make a hard
and a partly false distinction between those things
which he has to do and those things which he is disposed to do. He may not see that he is sometimes
disposed to do the things that he has to do (though
he may not be disposed to do them when he is constrained by the world to do them); he may even fail to
see that he has to do some of the things which he is
disposed to do (that his world would insist upon his
doing those things if he neglected them, though it is

unwilling for him to do them so often or for so long a time as he would, in an unfettered choice, elect).

He thus becomes an economist of time and of opportunity; he lays by a reserve, he begins as it were to bank his time and his opportunity; he builds up a margin. Here is real experimentation. He has learned that certain results follow certain actions, and that certain results are peremptorily demanded both by himself and by his world; but, when he has wraught those results, his day is not over. He has time and strength left, and in that time and with that strength he can not only achieve other results to which he knows the road, the road namely of actions which he has frequently repeated, but can attempt actions in this direction and in that, feeling his way cautiously or perhaps recklessly, moving along roads hitherto untried. But experiments of this kind are in value and character quite different from those others which he made before he knew either that certain actions have certain results or that he himself and his world demand those results. He may delight, and in general he does delight, in doing the known actions which bring known results; but he must do them whether he delights in them or not at the time when he and his world call for them to be done.

Virtue is its own reward; but virtue expresses itself in virtuous actions; or, if "action" is too gross and material a word, let us then say, in virtuous conduct, and, if conduct is too prosaic and offers itself too readily to external measurement and appraisal, then we may substitute for it "activity," which we are told may be inward or outward. The distinction is for our present purpose meaningless. If virtue be a principle, a moving force, then it makes for a result. It is not pedantic to note a difference between a good intention and a good performance. The world cannot command a good intention from children or for that matter from adult citizens; it can and does command certain good performances. Aristotle rightly said that a man does not deserve to be called grammatical merely because what he writes and speaks is grammatical: more than this is required, he must write and speak in a grammatical spirit. But we do not bid children write and speak in a grammatical spirit; we insist by precept, aided by example, and enforced by the very real sanction of not being understood, upon grammatical forms of writing and of speech. Out of the abundance of practice rules may be drawn, general maxims or regulations, and from these later the spirit of grammar may be evoked by some but probably not by all persons who have learned to use a language with correctness.

We need not deny that the mistakes of children are often pretty, and sometimes even useful to themselves as well as to the psychologists whose number appears to be rapidly increasing in the world; we may even admit that the mistakes and not less the successful attempts of children in the difficult exercise of speech may be called experiments, trials designed at one stage to discover what effect, if any, certain words and groupings of words will have upon the listeners, and, at another stage, if the result of the experiment has gratified those who made it, to discover whether these or those words or groupings of words repeated will bring again a desired effect. There is an earlier stage at which their words and wordless sounds are designed without reference to any other listeners, but for the gratification and easement of the speakers themselves, and a still earlier when sounds and the earliest words are uttered with little if any more intention than a sneeze or a cough upon the appropriate stimulus.

Now children must pass through these stages; they enjoy the passage, if it is not too much prolonged; older persons and parents are contented and perhaps proud witnesses of their children's passage through these stages, again upon the condition that they are not prolonged unduly; and it is to save trouble to themselves and their children that parents either directly or through the agency of other (and perhaps better equipped) adults teach them to talk and in good time to write. In every family every child in his "experiments" hits upon new modes of expression which are hailed with pious joy by their parents; but let the family be numerous and the parents comfortably honest, and they will tell each other, the contented father and the contented mother, that the new mode of their youngest reminds them of the mode now (thank God ! they sigh) abandoned by their eldest child. This originality, they remark, must be in the family. And they treasure this belief jealously and stoutly maintain it, though every other father and every other mother of their acquaintance proclaim the same originality for every other brood of children, and maintain it with a conviction which matches their own. Parents are now beginning to read the books of experimental psychologists and of teachers, who believe that children can teach themselves. When they have read in those works that the children of north and south, east and west, poor children, rich children, fair and dark, tall and short, will betray the originality, the inventiveness of their own, they will still, in face of all evidence, believe that there is something more original in the originality of their John and their Jemima; perhaps they will call it aboriginal, perhaps not.

We all make exceptions in favour of our own children and our own pupils. But surveying the children and the pupils of other folk we shall soon be compelled to see and to confess that there is a wonderful sameness in their originality, and that the range of their experiments is limited. The field of their exploration is circumscribed and hedged about: its area is fixed by two main determinant forces. The first is the weakness of the children themselves; their pretty playful expeditions and excursions are brought to a quick end by their inability to travel far from their base; they soon become tired and frightened and hurry home; the second is the foresight of their parents, who will not suffer them, when their untried courage would tempt them further, to go beyond the paddock, to overleap the fences. Often the parents are wrong in making the paddock too small, often in making the fences too stiff and too high. But in general they are right. They permit, they encourage, experiments within safe limits, experiments which may be conducted without too much cost to the children and to themselves. It is because the children enjoy a general safety and are protected as well as limited by the conditions set for them that they exhibit the confidence which their elders observe. Where this general safety is less complete we are ready to deplore the misfortune of the children and to decry the negligence of their parents. There is nothing which moves our pity so readily as the spectacle of children nervous and apprehensive of danger because they cannot trust a protection supplied to them by the providence of their elders.

Most children, we are fain to believe, can trust their elders; they climb, they fall; they fall as fearlessly as they climb, because they are sure enough that they will not be allowed to fall too heavily or too hard. They climb the same trees again and again; they fall frequently, until at last they have learnt to fall on their feet. These experiments they make at will, though within a limited range; there are other activities, which may not improperly be called experiments, to which they are urged and in which they are guided by their elders. A young student in a chemical laboratory claims that he is performing an experiment when into a test tube containing a specified quantity of a he pours a specified quantity of b. The result of adding a to b he may very likely have been told beforehand; he is verifying for himself what his teachers have long ago established by earlier experi-

ments, which themselves may have been of the nature
rather of verification than of discovery. Long ago
perhaps either genius or accident first combined *a*
and *b*. Now many activities of children, which we
sometimes call free, have the freedom of genius or of
accident, but of genius or accident insured against
too heavy a cost. They are experiments conducted
as it were under a guarantee; and it must be remembered that no rational guarantor accepts un-
limited responsibility. But there are other activities
in which children engage, not unwillingly, and yet
under compulsion, and these also may be called experiments in as much as, when the children first
engage in them, they are unable to guess or with
certainty to foretell the consequences. The consequences are known perfectly or for practical purposes
sufficiently well by their parents and teachers, though
they are not always explained in advance to the
children, who may have the lesson of surprise, when
that lesson has been long since learned by their elders.
If a student who has been told to add so much, a
specified quantity, of *a* to so much, a specified quantity, of *b*, under certain conditions, produces not *c*
but *z*, his teacher is, I believe, far more likely to
conclude that the student has made a mistake in his
measurements, or in his estimate of the conditions
in which the "experiment" should be made than to
congratulate the student in having made a discovery.
And the teacher will, I believe, cause the student to
make the same experiment over and over again, not
in the expectation, though not ruling out the possi-

bility, of the student's finding out some new thing, but with the intention of making the student accurate in manipulation, in observation, and in recording what he has done and seen. This is exactly our procedure, and this is our purpose in ordering and directing activities of children and young people in lessons which are not ordinarily called scientific, and in the affairs of every-day life. Certain results, known by us to be produced by certain causes operating in certain conditions, are desired by us for ourselves and for them.

Of these results we may agree that some are less important than others; but of some of them we shall say that they are essential and necessary, and therefore that the processes by which they are attained must be performed with a rigorous accuracy. Accuracy children may acquire by repetition, which is indeed not uncongenial to them. They love to play their old games without change; they are strongly conservative; they hate innovation, though it need hardly be remarked that the objects of their conservative devotion change with successive periods of their development in relative importance, and that the new thing which they hate to-day may to-morrow become an object of curiosity, and later either of indifference or of affection. By doing over and over again the things they want to do they learn to do them perfectly, and then to do them thoughtlessly, and so pass on to a stage at which they may be content to omit them altogether, but to omit them because some new things, some fresh activities have come to take the place of the old in their minds.

Now the vacant place is made by the mechanical perfection with which old processes have come to be performed. To this subject we shall soon revert. We have first to emphasise afresh a distinction which has been already drawn. It is this: some of the activities in which by repetition they freely attain perfection the world permits; some of the activities in which they are bound to attain perfection the world demands. The first fall within the region of *may*; the second fall within the region of *must*. It is when children begin to appreciate this distinction that they begin to perceive the distinction between work and play, and they know neither work nor play till they know at least that there is a difference between the two, though they may not be able in clear language to state what it is. The process of doing anything may be called a technique, but the word is applied more correctly, though not exclusively, to the process of doing anything which can be called a business, a craft, or an art. The analogy would not be violently disputed, but most persons would feel that an analogy was being used by a man who should speak of the technique of a game. A person who has mastered a technique has learnt perfectly to perform the several successive stages of a process. And he has reached perfection, as we say (very truly), when he can do what has to be done without thinking. He can now do it with a minimum of trouble, and his saving, his economy, is a saving, an economy of mental or physical labour.

But to have saved labour and to have saved time

is to have made leisure and to possess the energy with which to enjoy and use it. There are two ways in which we use leisure; we use it partly for doing other things than those which we are obliged to do; and we use it for turning to fresh purposes the things which we are constrained to do. "Work first and play afterwards" is a sound maxim; "Work while you work and play while you play" is another equally sound. "He is the freeman whom the truth makes free" is a third. For man there is no truth except truth of workmanship, the truth which he wins by toil. A man who has made a wheel which runs true, or has got some dovetailing true, or has compacted an argument and made it true, has achieved a freedom. He is then entitled to play. A man who can form letters with a pen easily and perfectly has achieved truth in that operation, and with it has won freedom. He is now entitled to play with his pen. A man who can speak with clearness and accuracy is now at liberty, he is free to pursue elegance; he may discover that the elegance with which he plays gives a new force, a finer precision, to his language; he turns language which he had mastered for his former purposes to new and higher purposes. Having learnt to speak the common language so as to say what he *means*, he discovers style; and he pursues and perhaps overtakes and captures style, with the result now at last of revealing what he *is*.

A man who has mastered a technique is the master of convention. A convention is a recognition of an end or purpose desired and the approval of the pro-

cesses necessary for attaining it. There are some conventions recognised by all men; the world insists upon
our keeping them or imposes penalties which may not
be shirked. One such convention, the widest in its
application, though it may be fulfilled in various
ways, is that if we are to live we must earn our living.
There are other conventions of narrower range; the
conventions of a particular nation, or group, or
society; these we must observe if we are to be permitted to live in or to enjoy the benefits of that
nation, group, or society. And we may without impropriety say that there are conventions which a man
makes with himself, and which he must keep if he
is to live in that small yet important and indeed
infinite universe which he calls himself.

As far as a man has mastered the technique of
living in his world, his group, and himself, he has
mastered the convention of each; he can survey his
world, his group, himself with eyes which leisure rests
and makes clear. No longer a slave to himself, his
group, or his world, he can break down the barriers
between them, because he sees over them. But he
must accept the conventions of each first, and acquire
the technique of each and then claim, and use his
freedom to criticise, to readjust, to re-interpret them.

CHAPTER XI

OURSELVES AND OUR NEIGHBOURS

" AND" though it looks so simple and little is the
most potent and fertile of words.

Let it fasten itself to anything in the world, it is
ready to associate that thing with anything and
everything else.

The association which it forms may be that of mere
addition as when field is joined to field and house to
house. It may be that of partnership and co-operation
as when one man allies himself with another so that
together they may achieve a common purpose, or gets
for himself the aid of a slave, a horse or an inanimate
instrument to do what unaided it would be idle for
him to attempt. Or once more it may be that of
contrast and opposition when forces alien to or irreconcilable with each other are made to meet. This
word which we call a conjunction, which seems to
serve the plain purpose of connecting one thing with
another, serves also to mark every kind of distinction.
So when we maintain that there are grapes and grapes
we may mean that there are grapes and more grapes
of the same kind, but the slightest stress upon the
conjunction will indicate to those who hear us that
there are good grapes and bad, sweet and bitter,
within our reach or inaccessible.

Ourselves and our neighbours are linked together
by this slender but quite indissoluble bond. Together

we and they make up the world, a world of alliances
and affinities, of differences and varieties, of friend-
ships and hatreds, of simple wholeness and of distracting separations, of reconciliation and estrangement. "And" is the common sign which all these
modes of relationship carry, it is the enigmatic mask
which they all wear. Only one thing we may say con-
fidently about the word; it never stands for identity,
there can be no relationship where there is identity;
and since significance rests upon relationship, we may
say that identity can not be asserted in an intelligible
and intelligent world.

The first remark we have to make about our neighbours is that they are other than ourselves. Our senses
are the avenues by which we approach them and by
which they on their part essay communication with
us, but they are avenues which we can block or cut
off. We see our neighbours; but rich as is the gift of
sight, not less precious is the power to shut our eyes:
we hear their voices, receiving delight from some and
distress from others; but we can stop our ears; we
smell and taste and touch, but the nostril may be
gratified or affronted, the palate quickened or cloyed,
the sensitive flesh soothed or tortured, and against
the monotony of pleasure or the prolongation of pain,
we have our remedy; we may bar the road, and shut
ourselves up. Not completely, it may be said; escape
is not so easy: granted, but escape may at least be
sought, and often won; and when we find ourselves
imprisoned in a world from which there is no outlet,
we note the more accurately the discrepancy be-

tween it and ourselves. And there is sleep, when we are assailed either not at all or by other engines than those which the world uses upon us in our waking hours. And there is death, which some have conceived to be sleep, oblivion and mere nothingness, though most men probably regard it as a door into a condition of which yet we have no knowledge except that we are to pass through it—we ourselves, and so carry beyond its blind front the habit of distinguishing which has grown to be our very nature. In another world, we shall find ourselves, other than that world, and shall be confronted once more with the problem of ourselves and our neighbours. Having once noted that our neighbours, our nearest, are other than ourselves—and in parenthesis it may be hinted that the differences are most easily and most constantly observed when the neighbours are very near—we hasten at a stride to the conclusion that we are better, or at any rate more important than, they.

Birth is a violent estrangement by which what was one life becomes two; and presently, as soon as we declare that the still speechless infant takes notice, we give it to be understood that he for his part has given notice that he has now consciously separated himself from the arm which holds him, and draws his nourishment from an alien, because a kindred, source. Kinship is the sharpest edge of difference, and is itself a discovery of which the poignant meaning reveals itself in the slow passage of the years bringing pain outlined by pleasure and pleasure shot with pain, a distinction once again, which marks

otherness. For him, that child, the world which he
finds set over against him is his mother; to know that
he is near her is to know that he is himself and she
not himself, and he learns the closeness of their union
when he discovers for the first time that she is near
no longer. He then distinguishes between unity, which
would negate his own life, and that union which implying separation fulfils both his and hers. But the
word fulfil, just used, must be at once withdrawn; let
us rather say that his awareness of alliance is a condition, one of many that are to follow, the first and
perhaps the best, of the fulfilment of a life which is
to bear many relations. For the terror of loneliness
resides in the fact that the terrified spirit perceives
that it is not alone; it has lost touch with that part
of the world to which it had grown accustomed, and
is looking with unfamiliar eyes into the face of an
unfamiliar world, the language of which it cannot
understand and to which it has no intelligible language to utter. It is the condition of a lost soul in a
universe to which it is not adjusted. The condition,
intolerable both to the individual and to the world,
is brought to an end by the establishment of new
relations, the shock of sheer surprise being itself a
relation, succeeded by fear, and fear by dawning hope
and hope by trust; terms are made, a new language
is forged to embody them.

The world which was once made up of himself and
his mother from whom he drew and by whose ministrations he maintains his life is now tripartite: a third
member has been added; his world now consists of

himself, first as ever, his mother, and an undifferentiated remainder. But the analysis by which he has already enlarged his range is not to stop at this point: the experience of an immortal life is the process by which we analyse the remainder. And the reason is precisely that which we have already observed. Analysis is forced upon the child as upon the man, because he seeks to establish intelligible relationships with a world which he finds confronting him; he must divide to rule; he must interpret in order to use; he must put a new construction, if you will an ideal construction, upon the confused and threatening mass which is over against him. From it, he sorts out his nurse, his father, his brothers and sisters, the servants of the house, his school-fellows and teachers and the rest. And what is the method and the result of his sifting? The sifting is nothing else than the continuous discovery of the uses which these people have for him, and the result is in the fact that he does indeed make use of them.

The result, we have said; but once again a correction must be made, a proviso laid down. It is the result only for that blameless egotist whom we call a baby: let this result be all when he shall have grown even to boyhood, and if we call him an egotist we no longer call him blameless: but we do not call him an egotist, we call him a selfish pig, doing a gross injustice to one of the most useful of animals. For the truth is that to use the world, and in especial to use those persons in it with whom we have clearly recognised relations, we must contribute to its uses.

It is not a question necessarily or primarily of bargaining; the issue is deeper than that; to use is to participate in the life of the things or persons we use, and in so doing to make them or suffer them to be participants in ours. The pig savouring the contents of the swill pail is preparing himself to adorn the human table; he comes home to us at that critical hour when, secluded from the outer world, we eat the morning bacon in the silence of our families, he touches a note of pathos and of magnificence in the orchestra of a feast, when he lays his own head as a crown upon a banquet. He pays his way. The infant gives unwittingly to his parents and his keepers; he provides them with an object of affection, a theme for conversation, and, while he makes them into a gymnasium for his growing muscles, is himself a vaulting-horse for their ambition, a field for the exercise of their patience; he is at once the pledge and the test of their plighted love.

But infancy stretched beyond its pretty and proper span (too short, we say, but long enough) is disaster for the child and destruction for his parents. He must receive more, and more special, services from them and from the world; but he must give more, and give knowingly. He classifies the world according to the intimacy and the richness of the services which he receives from various people, and also according to the return which he is now able to make to them. The process is continued through life; and if ever we say of people that we have no use for them, the sentence means that we cannot make or are unwilling

to continue relationships with them. When childhood
has passed away and youth has followed it and both
are become a memory and a tradition, we find ourselves grown to maturity, and measure ourselves by
the number, the variety, the wealth of the associa-
tions which we have set up. These may be divided
into three groups; we have our place in the general
world, but what we give to it and receive from it we
but dimly perceive, though the exchange is continuous
while we live; then we have our place in a narrower
world within that larger whole, and here our relationships are either clearly perceived, sometimes indeed
because we have ourselves deliberately set them up
or because they have been forced upon us, or deeply
and dumbly understood, when they are so long established and so perfect in their working that we need
hardly think about them; and, last, we have our
place in that most restricted circle of all, of our close
friends or our families—a circle with the members of
which we have both close and constant association:
and here we have a perfectly mechanical and a me-
chanically perfect interchange of services, and also
that imperfect, because growing, understanding which
gives to life its shocks and surprises.

This contradiction at the very heart of intimacy
may be illustrated by a simple example. We are all
so well accustomed to the faces and the voices, to the
attitudes, gesture, gait of our nearest kindred or our
partners in daily work that for the most part we may
say properly that we do not notice them; but one day
our eye will fall upon a very strange face, and the

sharpness of our wonder will come from the fact that
it is not a strange face at all, but that of a friend, the
same and yet different; an unfamiliar voice will greet
or arraign us, and we shall hear beneath the new
note the ghost of a voice that we have heard a
thousand times, the living dead striving with the
deadly living; that pose, that play of the hand,
that movement—each is new and the newness is cruel
with the sharpened edge of a once blunted familiarity.

The boundaries between these several worlds of our
life's commerce are, to be sure, not hard set; they
change—from the great general world we draw to our
use some fresh element, or are ourselves caught up
into untried modes of dealing with it; and on the
other hand we may lose or allow to fall into neglect
some of our negotiations with that inner and that
inmost region of our nearer and nearest comrades
and partners and friends and kindred. Our speech
with the members of each group is, as it must needs
be, determined by the things which we desire to say
to them and hear from them; our conversation depends upon our needs and our power to meet answering needs which they feel and express. But what
we are doing in all this business is to preserve our own
life, to make good, to realise ourselves. And within
each group we make distinctions as between the
groups themselves, only finer and more accurate distinctions. We seek this man because he can supply
what we want and what we get from no other; we
seek a second and a third and every one for the like
reason; to appease a hunger, to quench a thirst, at

a source from which we have learnt that our appetite can be satisfied. True, in satisfying ourselves, we must make a contribution to the life of those others upon whose resources we draw. But need, needs, variety of needs, insistent, irresistible drive us to our fellows, and we distinguish between them according to what they give us. Not from all do we look to get the same things; else we were surfeited and starved at once. Not an equal value do we set upon the several benefits which we draw from our so various neighbours; we have our preferences: if a choice must be made, this we will have and that we will forgo, and more of this and less of that is an everyday choice. But the choice is made in reference to ourselves; we classify, we arrange, we have an order of merit which we bestow or inflict upon a world which is putting us also in our place, exercising its own preferences and passing its judgment.

In brief, an enlightened self-interest is our guide. We need not pause here to wonder, if our light be darkness, how great that darkness must be. We shall have occasion presently to make something more than an exclamation in this matter. Let us rather note that, while we are sorting the world and determining the classes into which we divide its inhabitants according to the nature of the supplies which we get from them, as a geographer colours an economic map showing that here coal is found and here iron, here wheat grows, and there are grass lands, at the same time we are mapping out ourselves. We have not one general want, but many and various wants, and we

arrange these in an order or indeed in several orders
of interest and importance. We need beef and we
need books; which shall we place higher, that element
in us which calls for beef or that other which hungers
for books? We may spend more time in earning our
bodily food than in building up our libraries; and very
likely more time in eating our meals than in reading.
Let us set three hours a day as a reasonable time for
eating; how many people are there who read regularly
every day for the same number of hours? Or, once
more, we need money and society; and we spend
more time in getting money than in enjoying society.
It is not contended that the length of time which we
spend upon the pursuit of an object is the sole or even
a principal criterion of the value which we set upon
it in comparison with other objects; but it is one
criterion. And, however the decision may fall, our
argument remains the same, and it is a very simple
one; that some of our desires we admit to be more
imperious or nobler than others, and some of our
objects more necessary or better than others.

Let us now turn back for a moment from ourselves
to the world, and we cannot deny that, when we
classify people according to the services which they
render, and when we without hesitation declare that
some objects, or services rendered, are nobler and
better or more necessary than others, we have perhaps
unintentionally, but quite effectively, drawn class
distinctions in the world, distinctions which mark off
from one another the various groups with which we
have dealings in accordance with the functions exer-

cised by each. We learnt long ago that A is an apothecary, B is a butcher or a baker, C is a candle-stick-maker, P is a ploughboy, T a tinker or a tailor, S a soldier or a sailor. By their fruits we know them, that is, by their works, their services, and we may add their disservices, for we recall that T may be a thief. Now barring the last-named, who however has always found a foothold in the world, we realise that we have need of all these people, and call on them for services, but not on all of them for the same services; and regarding some of the services as more important or more honourable than others we arrange or at least are disposed to arrange the men who render the various services in an order of preference.

This order is subject indeed to some changes; for example, the butcher and the baker may usually play a larger part for us than the apothecary, but on a rare occasion his part may be more important than theirs; or it may be argued that, though we less con-stantly need the services which he is prepared to render, yet the extremity of our need for them when the need happens to exist compels us to accord him a place of permanent superiority to that which they enjoy. Or, once more, one man may love music and have no interest in painting, another may be an amateur of pictures and have no use for music; the one will set the musician, the other the painter, high in order; the order, that is, of his own preference and use. Yet both will agree to set the painter and the musician higher in the scale of value or use than the dustman, though they might live without music or pictures and could not live without the ministrations of the dustman.

If our argument has carried us so far, it must carry us to a further and more intimate distinction. If we classify other people in accordance with the uses which they fulfil for us, it is clear that we discover within ourselves a variety of appetites or elements or parts to which these many several persons render services. We regard some of our needs as higher than others, and so we say that some elements in ourselves are superior to others. We recognise a series of grades; we speak of our better selves, or our lower selves; we distinguish between body and mind, and profess to set the body lower than the mind; and when we consider either body or mind we are ready to grant differences, the body must be fed and clothed and housed and here are three several services which are rendered to it, and each of these may be rendered with or without good taste or comfort. The mind must be supplied with food and exercise; it also must have a habitation and be clothed; but there is good and ample food for the mind, or good and insufficient, or bad and plentiful, and the like distinctions may be made in regard to the mind's furniture, equipment, and dwelling.

To be sure our practice may not correspond with our profession; if geniality is the note which we wish to strike and believe we hit, it would shock us to be told that our god is our belly; but the accusation might justly be made; and if we on our side charged a neighbour with too devoted a care for material things, he might reply that in the selection of his carpets, the ordering of his wines, the choice of his silver, or the cut of his clothes, he was proving himself a scrupulous artist and exercising a disciplined imagination; and he might speak truly, though we should be more readily disposed to believe this if it were said of him than by him.

Yet, whatever variations there may be in the order in which we place our fellows, and in that other but comparable, if not quite parallel, order in which we place the elements into which we divide ourselves, there is a tolerable fixity in our judgments and a tolerable agreement between our judgments and those of our neighbours. We agree to put some people above others, and are satisfied that the superior dignity should be marked by wealth or social consideration or both. But here we come upon a bewildering problem. We saw just now that T may be a tinker or a tailor, and were sadly forced to own that T might even be a thief. Let us turn the sentence round; let us rather declare what we see when unmasked and even threateningly it turns itself round. We see then that the tinker, the tailor, and the thief are all T. They are all different, but this simple letter proclaims them related. They have all a common name; look, it is a family name; it is our family name; they are all men. It is a bewildering, a disturbing thought. We may love our kindred; but we do not brook the claim of all men to be our kindred; their name is legion, and the word has its strong and accepted association. It would seem that, in their main quality, these human creatures whom we have been at the pains to sort out into classes and to arrange in an order, corresponding to certain familiar functions which they render—that in their main quality they are all alike, and more than that, all one. The delicate, discerning mind shrinks in horror from the conclusion. What is to be done? Cannot we restore the happy differences which sundered class from class, profession from profession, and the world in general from that supremely interesting and individual part of it which we call ourselves? May we not say that functions match dispositions and are indicated by nature herself? We shall comfortably acquiesce in a system which puts one man upon the box of a brougham to drive through a November sleet and another man inside the carriage, because we persuade ourselves that one is by nature a coachman and the other by nature a proprietor. Willing slaves of the same argument, we learn to tolerate ourselves; it is natural for us to do, to have, to be whatever we do, have and are; we are what we are as clearly as our neighbours are what they are, and shall be content if they will keep their place.

CHAPTER XII

UNITY AND DIFFERENCE

EVERY man, we say, has his proper place; and we deserve a good place. The doctrine has much to commend it; there is much of truth in it; indeed, in its general statement it is quite true; but when it is applied numerous difficulties appear. First, assuming that our own place is decently comfortable, we remark that our neighbours are stubbornly unwilling to remain in the place which we think so well fitted to their gifts, a place subordinate to our own; or, assuming on the contrary that we are ill content with our own place, we find that our neighbours, now on the other side, are hostile to any efforts which we may put forth for ousting them—planting ourselves in a position for which we are sure they are not fit, and which would admirably become us. Indeed, both these assumptions may be made; envied by some, we envy others; and we may compare the revolutions of society either to that childish game where everyone is moving on and on to seize a chair before another takes it, and which is brought to an end by the removal at last of the chairs themselves, or, more grossly, we may liken it to the roughest scrimmage. These are difficulties; but there is another. Silent, but irrepressible, is the protest of our hearts against the system: when we have forced our way to the sheltered corner and the comforting fire, a chill seizes

us as we reflect upon those others, so like us though
on our own assumption so little deserving of what we
have got, who are out in the cold; or, if we are shut
out from the welcoming glow, we are hot with indignation at the sight, through hard transparent windows,
of those who have won what we have sought in vain.
There is an incurable sympathy in human nature, and
an incurable rivalry. Those also, we cry, are men,
flesh and blood, no worse than ourselves, as we look
upon the starving and the destitute; those also are
men, flesh and blood and no better than ourselves,
as we look upon those who are sleek with prosperity.
We clamour, or sigh, for equality. It is an amiable
weakness; it is superb folly. Mr Chesterton provides
an eloquent example in the beautiful essay which he
has seen fit to entitle *A Short History of England*—
a work not the less highly to be praised because the
truth he reaches is poetic rather than merely historical, the truth, that is to say, of a creator rather
than that of a collector; and not the less carefully
to be scrutinised because some of his utterances have
the deceptive glitter of half truths rather than the
serene and simple light of plain facts.

Let us listen to him[1]

Say the very word "Equality" in many modern countries, and four hundred fools will leap to their feet at once
to explain that some men can be found, on careful examination, to be taller or handsomer than others. As if
Danton had not noticed that he was taller than Robes-
pierre, or as if Washington was not well aware that he
was handsomer than Franklin. This is no place to expound

[1] p. 202.

a philosophy; it will be enough to say in passing, by way of a parable, that when we say that all pennies are equal, we do not mean that they all look exactly the same, we mean that they are absolutely equal in their one absolute character, as the most important thing about them. It may be put practically by saying that they are coins of a certain value, twelve of which go to a shilling. It may be put symbolically, and even mystically, by saying that they all bear the image of the King. And, though most mystical, it is also the most practical summary of equality that all men bear the image of the King of Kings.

This is excellent rhetoric; we have no complaint to make of it; it serves Mr Chesterton's wholly laudable purpose. But we must agree with him when he assures us that he is not expounding a philosophy, and we agree the more surely because we know that he calls people who do not agree with him very dull fellows. And yet we may allow ourselves to feel and to express surprise and regret that an author who can command so many analogies, similes and metaphors, and is not afraid to crowd upon a single page or to pack into a single sentence images which startle the reader by their apparent incongruity has here been niggardly and offered us but one. Indeed, if he had been more lavish in his illustrations, Mr Chesterton might on this occasion have been more philosophical.

Let us repeat, with his main contention we agree; we are wholly of his opinion; but for practical guidance he leaves us sadly to seek. Pennies have a certain value; but have men? And, if they have, surely it is determined not only by the superscription which is written upon their foreheads, but by the functions which they serve. One penny is as good as another, because it serves the same function; but men differ in their functions, and if one man is to be regarded as being as good as another it must be for some other reason. Mr Chesterton leaves us in no doubt as to this other reason, but he does not help us to discover what we need to discover, namely, the relation of variety of function to unity or similarity in value. And he assures us that twelve pennies make a shilling: once again we are heartily with him. But how many men, or how many groups of men, make a society? Moreover, we recall the threepenny piece, and we still see the sixpenny bit; are we to say that each of these is equal to the other and also to the penny, because all bear the same image of the King? In the sight of God all men may be equal; but for the work of the world all men are not equal, and their inequality is measured by two tests: if several men are engaged in the same occupation, say, pianoforte playing, we shall not be convicted of stupidity or of inhumanity when we say that one is better than another, even if we are wrong in our opinion as to which is really the best: the best is he who does that thing, in the judgment either of ourselves or of a majority of listeners, or of some critic accredited with authority, better than the others: that is one test, applied to several competitors in a single field of activity. We use the other when we compare different fields of activity, thus we say that, while A is a first-rate cricketer, he is not so good as B at football; and the fact that A is good at cricket and B at football we refuse to take as evidence

that either of them is as good as *C* at the piano, or that
either of them has any ability at all in playing on that
instrument. We differentiate men according to the skill
and the success with which they do their work, and
also according to the nature of the work which they do.

A more fertile analogy, fertile like all analogies both
in crops of error and in harvests of truth, is that of
a complicated machine. The machine as a whole is
designed for some purpose and as a whole it works
towards the fulfilment of that purpose. But the
success of its total or general operation depends upon
a fine adjustment of parts which serve several special
ends, related to each other, but different from one
another, and having as their one common attribute
or quality the fact that they are all subordinate to
an end which is other and greater than the performance of their several parts. Indeed, the difference
between them is expressed by their relationship, and,
even when we say that the perfect working of every
part is necessary and essential to the working of the
whole, we shall not be taken to mean that a small
screw is as valuable or important as a boiler or a
dynamo. The simplest household contains many instruments and utensils of rare or frequent use; some
are for honour and some for dishonour. The simplest
household involves a variety of labour; no part of it
need be for dishonour, but no part of it is the same
as another or intended to meet the same needs. A man
does his work, his wife does hers, the servants, the
children have their proper rôles; and the most settled
balance, the best ordered harmony is kept and pre-

served when they find and remain in their proper
places.

Efficiency was not many years ago set up before
us as an ideal. If the word means a condition of
perfect fitness for the performance of a function
specially suited to the gifts of any person, it needs
little argument to show that with efficiency we must
claim co-ordination. No one man can do the very
thing for which he is supremely well adapted by
nature and discipline if other people insist on doing
the same thing at the same time in the same place;
but co-ordination is only another name for subordination; the arrangement of persons and powers
in an order designed for the achievement of a common
end by many different agents. Justice, according to
Plato, was simply that; the performance by each
individual, and each group in a state or society, of
the work appropriate to him or it. Justice is exhibited, it is indeed brought into being and preserved,
by every man's minding his own business. Now here
is the crux of the practical problem: how is the special
business of each person to be discovered by himself
or by others? If he discovers it himself, will he be
permitted to do it? If others discover it for him, how
can they convince him that they have truly divined
his gifts and so justly determined his function? They
must convince him: merely to force him would be to
defeat their own purpose. Plato, we remember, makes
two assumptions, or rather lays down two premises.
He makes no question that some services and the
gifts which are necessary for their rendering are su-

perior to other services and gifts. He does not, of course, declare that these superior gifts and services are to be exercised or fulfilled without reference to other lower gifts and services: indeed, it is impossible to call anything or any person superior unless we compare him or it to an inferior; in its measure and in its place the inferior serves the superior as the superior serves it. And all the several elements of a state or society are bound together by the co-ordinated but differentiated services which each renders to the whole.

That is the first premise; his second is like it, but much harder of acceptance. He assumes, in the second place, that men will recognise these actual differences which separate only to associate them; that *A* will readily agree both that his gifts are other than those of *B* and that they are inferior to his, and that *B* will admit not unwillingly that he is the superior of *A*. Not unwillingly will he grant this, but not hastily; for to admit superior gifts is to accept graver responsibilities and to undergo an ascetic training.

These gifts are natural, but they are to be discovered and proved by trial and perfected by a stern and lifelong discipline. The governors, the rulers, are nobly called "consummate artificers of liberty[1]," and it is clear that liberty is that exact co-ordination, that easy recognition of duty and of rank corresponding with duty which enables the members and classes of a composite society to cleave together. To keep these men from the danger of forgetting, for-

[1] *Republic* III, 395 c. See Bosanquet, *Education of the Young in the* Republic *of Plato*.

saking, and forswearing their supreme function they must be subjected to trials. From childhood tasks must be set them "in which a man might most readily forget or be deluded out of" the principle which is at the heart of liberty, the principle of order. Only those who can meet this test successfully are to be continued in training for the high profession of statesmanship. And there is the further test of hard work and of pain; they must learn to endure both. Lastly, there is the test of sudden encounter with terrors and pleasures, both of which may exercise a witchery over the mind, and soften it. They must be strong to resist these influences. All these proofs they must give in advance; and in the end, when they have entered on their office, we must see, says Socrates, what manner of life we desire them to live, if they are to maintain their character and discharge their function. This is the manner of their life,

first, none of them possessing any property of his own, except what is absolutely necessary; then, none to have any house or store-chamber into which all cannot enter when they please; and their provisions, all that men need who are experts in warfare, temperate and brave, they are to receive on a settled estimate from the rest of the citizens as the wages of their guardianship, to such an amount that in every year there shall be neither surplus or deficit; and to live in common like men in camp, having their meals together, and for gold and silver, we must tell them that they have these always in their souls, divine and god-given, and have no need of what men call such beside...for them alone of all that are in the city it is not allowable to handle gold and silver, nor to go under the same roof with it, nor to wear ornaments of it, nor to drink out of silver and gold....And so they would be safe, and save their city[1].

This is the training, this the manner of life of those who are fit to rule; but those whom they rule, the military class and the productive or trading class, including every kind of artist and artificer, must be ready to perfect themselves for their several tasks by an exclusive and lifelong devotion to them. It is not necessary to do more than remind ourselves in passing that Plato makes provision by which a child, who by nature belongs to one class but is by chance born in another, is put up or down into the class to which he can properly lay claim, his title being proved by his ability to render certain distinctive services. What is to be remarked as the central doctrine is that services are rendered not so much by individuals to individuals or by this class to that, as by all individuals and all classes to the total, to the society in which they live and move and have their being, and which in its turn springs into existence and continues to live in virtue of their co-ordinated activities. It is this which gives dignity, a sufficient but not the same dignity to all the active members of a society, and inactive members on this hypothesis cannot exist; the description is indeed a contradiction in terms.

We spoke earlier of an enlightened self-interest which would teach men to seek in one quarter for certain benefits and in another for others, and to pay back in mere and mercenary requital such balancing services as might be required. But self-interest cuts

---

[1] *Republic* III, 416 D, E; 417 A (see Bosanquet, *op cit.*).

the ground from under the feet of those who profess it and attempt to follow its guidance. There can be no life in a dismembered body; and a body articulated, compact of muscles and limbs, veins and arteries and organs of whatever kind is a total, the whole of which is affected by every operation of its constituent parts, while its constituent parts render service each to the rest through the total in relation to which alone they are parts and have significance. Thus it comes about that for any part to realise itself and indeed to be at all, it must needs lose itself in the other parts and in the whole, just as the whole only exists in the fulfilment and perfection of its constituents.

These words have now come to be so easy on our lips that the theory indicated by them is not examined with the care which it deserves and which it would receive if it could come fresh and sudden and shocking to the world. At least we should question it, and ask whether indeed self-sacrifice is self-realisation, or a condition and the only condition upon which it can be won. We should refuse the facile assent which means that with the feigned form of politeness we quite resolutely decline to entertain the question, much less to adopt the theory. And to look steadily at this question is to see that it cannot be answered with a plain acquiescence or a blunt denial. Truth is a blade of two edges; it cuts both ways; and we have to make the best of a difficult position in which language cannot give us the precise expression for what we come to believe. Self-sacrifice is not self-realisation; because in fact there is no self-

sacrifice in the service of society. Self-realisation is
not a goal at which we can properly aim; for, as has
been shown, to realise ourselves is to realise our
failures and our disabilities. Within the body of the
state or of society a process goes on exactly comparable with that which goes on within the body and
in the spiritual or mental experience of the individual.
The growth of a child from birth to maturity is a
process in which it discovers one after another its
own limbs and powers; while the discovery is new,
the child has incomplete but conscious use of these
limbs and exercise of these powers; while he has to
think in order to walk, and thinks that he is walking,
he walks stumblingly and uncertainly; it is only when
he can think (about something else) while he is walking
that he has fully learnt to walk. In other words, he
has then and only then learnt to do this very necessary
thing, when he has so perfectly co-ordinated the
operations of walking with those other operations,
with which they are associated or for the sake of
which they are undertaken, that he walks unconsciously. The actions which we perform in writing
illustrate the same fact. While we have to control
and direct the movement of our fingers with conscious
effort, we have not learnt to write; we have only
learnt to write when we write without knowing it,
intent on the purpose for the sake of which we undertake that laborious process. The perfect service of
the hand guiding the pen is a service in which the
hand moves unconsciously and is forgotten. Now,
though it may be said truly that the hand is sub-

ordinate to the mind the thoughts of which it traces on paper; yet, when the subordination is complete, when rivalry and opposition are impossible, when even polite and intentional co-operation is out of the question, then at last the hand and the mind are at one.

All this has been discerned and illuminated with his accustomed and steady brilliance by Samuel Butler in his *Life and Habit*. The paradox and the truism to which he leads us can best be put in his own words.

"It would appear," he writes, "as though perfect knowledge and perfect ignorance were extremes which meet and become indistinguishable from one another; so also perfect volition and perfect absence of volition, perfect memory and utter forgetfulness; for we are unconscious of knowing, willing, or remembering, either from not yet having known or willed, or from knowing and willing so well and so intensely as to be no longer conscious of either. Conscious knowledge and volition are of attention; attention is of suspense; suspense is of doubt; doubt is of uncertainty; uncertainty is of ignorance; so that the mere fact of conscious knowing or willing implies the presence of more or less novelty or doubt....In either case—the repose of perfect ignorance or of perfect knowledge—disturbance is troublesome....A uniform impression is practically no impression. One cannot either learn or unlearn without pains or pain[1]."

When we think about the nature of society it is very hard for us to figure to ourselves the repose either of perfect ignorance or of perfect knowledge; yet it is probably by a figure or a simile that we can come nearest to the meaning of these words and indeed

[1] *Op. cit.* Fifield, 1916, p. 18.

discover whether they convey a meaning or not. The simplest society is clearly one made up of several members, distinct from each other, though united by some invisible bonds or some unanalysed alchemy which makes them one. A basket full of young puppies might represent for us such a group or society. They come of the same stock, they are related one to another, but they are not conscious yet of relationship. A family of young children may be related in the same way, and yet unaware of their relationship; and both puppies and children may be completely comfortable and at rest in that condition of blissful ignorance. But the condition does not last long. The young creatures grow, and to grow is to learn and unlearn; it is to unlearn the habit of a primitive harmony; it is to learn the steps which must be taken in the direction of a new and hitherto unreached concord.

They suffer growing pains, and learn that here in them, of them, discernible but not separable, is a leg to be stretched, a tail to be wagged, an eye to turn beyond the edge of the basket and the limits of the home, upon a strange and untravelled world. Each one of those movements causes a double awareness, awareness of self and awareness of the world, of that little world to which at the moment it extends. And awareness brings a twofold discomfort; the growing creature becomes too large for the place in which he discovers himself; feeling the distressing pressure of his neighbours, he distresses them by his own presence, trespassing upon them.

This same family feeling already brings for puppies

and for children a sense of the difference between the group of which they are members and the rest of the world. The puppies know themselves to be alien from the kittens of the household; the children know themselves as a group to be different from and, they suspect, superior to the neighbour's children. But these increases of knowledge are all accompanied by a loss of stability of equilibrium: we are balancing and tottering and put out our hands upon our neighbours' shoulders, and they do as much for us. We learn to walk on our own legs, when we have broken up the happy rotundity of babyhood into those and other limbs and parts of the body; but at once we find that it is not on our own legs that we walk, or in our own strength; we quickly see that we are ourselves parts of a larger body, limbs in it, organs of it; and the fact that we are, as we say, aware of ourselves, is only a part of that larger fact that it, that total, has become aware of us, and is in the same action casting us forth and leaning upon us, using us.

It is very natural that we should think in terms of the individual, as we are wont to call him. Not to press further the argument that an individual does not deserve that singularly infelicitous name until he has in some measure at least divided himself into parts of which he is conscious and aware, let us rather note that what was said earlier about birth, must now be either recalled or corrected. We speak of birth as if it were the beginning of a new form of life, which detaches itself or is thrust forth from an older form. But we might equally well or better regard birth as

the emergence of a new consciousness in the old form
of life, which hitherto has not analysed itself into its
real components. Some rapidly drawn illustrations
may make this matter clear. When we speak of the
Renaissance, we commonly suppose ourselves to mean
the revival or the rebirth of classical studies in Europe,
and we are quite right in assigning this meaning to
the word; but we should be equally right if we declared that what we meant was a new life into which
Europe entered when it disentangled from its possessions a long disused treasure. Or, again, if we
speak of the discovery of a force like electricity or of
a star, we are prone to fix our notice on the thing
discovered as if it were new indeed: newly discovered
it certainly may be, but the discovery consisted in
an analysis more shrewd and accurate than any conducted hitherto into the total of the world in which
we already lived, and which contained the new thing
before we were aware of its existence.

It is the world which becomes new by a process
of self-analysis. The process must be traced back to
its origin, though for our purpose the origin must be
arbitrarily marked. We can imagine for ourselves,
or for a world or for any living whole, a condition of
quiescent satiety; but this condition passes away; it
is followed by hunger and the effort to appease hunger,
and a further effort to amass a store against need.
For nourishment to be absorbed reproduction is
necessary, we throw into our activities something of
ourselves; when we succeed in putting into our work
or our play more than we ordinarily give of ourselves

we call that work or play, that achievement or performance our creation, our child. We can stand away
from it, and criticise it; it is itself a critic and a criterion
of our vitality. The whole world is a great artificer,
a general parent, thrusting out its own life in ever
new manifestations or births of creative energy. The
whole creation groans and travails in this constant
task, self-imposed or natural, call it what we may,
of re-making itself. And the process is one of pain.
The offspring may or may not at first suffer agony,
the parent always does. But pain awaits the new life
too, and springs from the double effort of realising,
that is analysing itself, and of realising, that is once
more of analysing, its relation to the source from
which it sprang. The new reconstructs the old world
and becomes the parent of its progenitor. The child
is father of the man, because it makes the man a
father. It renders the like service to the mother.

We must not then be too much disheartened by
the troubles of the world. Certainly, we must admit
that there are dislocations and damages, malforma-
tions and other calamities; it is the office of government, that medical faculty in the state, to arrange,
to adjust, to correct these; but the very meaning of
healthy growth and development is the discovery
and the fashioning of relationships: until these are
fashioned there must ever be a want of harmony and
co-ordination, and the method of fashioning them is
nothing else than the discovery of them. To invent
is to create, to discover is to make. Polytheism is a
mode of apprehending the universe by which man,

discovering deity everywhere, breaks the silent and inarticulate unity of Godhead into a multitude of related persons who may speak one to another and, each in a special voice to match his special needs, to man. The divine solitude blossoms into a family. When the tedium of celestial domesticity wears the nerves of the gods in Olympus, Homer sends them upon a visit to the blameless Ethiopians, for the refreshment which comes from conversation, from the discovery and enjoyment of new relationships. Elsewhere we have the same fact proclaimed, the same lesson taught in other and subtler language. The word which was God is the word which was from God; the proof of his unity is the consciousness of himself made articulate in speech to the creatures with whom he is identified, and from whom to make that oneness real he must dissever himself.

Speech, the instrument of alliance, is the engine of definition; a treaty is set out in terms, and a perfect boundary is the invisible line which marks and makes sacred the vivid and throbbing connections of a differentiated and therefore unified life. Until the boundary has been perfectly drawn we attempt with skilled or clumsy fingers to trace it. We quarrel with what are called class distinctions; we should rather lament their obliteration. A map strewn with the names of provinces the limits of which are not understood and observed is a symbol of war. Within any society, large or small, distinction of class should stand for a system of interrelated services. Granted the names survive when the distinctions have been blurred. It is an

argument for renewing the vital distinctions, or re-
cognising new distinctions which shall correspond
with fresh and real relationships. It is an argument
for restoring unity, which is threatened and almost
destroyed by confusion. The power which can claim
to be Alpha and Omega, the beginning and the end,
is ever engaged in the work of creation, making all
things new by ever freshly arranging and distributing
its own powers. Creation begins at the end. Yet,
since imagination boggles at a thought so simple, we
make for ourselves, like writers of school histories, an
arbitrary starting-point.

Far back in unmeasured time, we say, in a solitary
world was a thing, the germ of life, but counter-
feiting death in its speechlessness and surpassing
death in its deathless stillness. Yet life it is and a
living thing, and it preys upon the world in which it
miserably and hungrily exists. It finds its nourishment, or rather absorbs what is provided for it; with
food it grows; it grows by gluttony and bursts with
repletion. Behold the one is become two, the two a
multitude. The patch of the universe which sustained
one is too narrow for the multitude, the food supply
is insufficient, and the innumerable offspring of that
elemental one are engaged in war upon their kindred.
Slaughter cannot keep the demand for food within
the limits of the supply, and perforce migration begins,
a search is made for new feeding-grounds. But these
are already tenanted, for the world which we supposed solitary had other, also speechless, inhabitants.
Accustomed to fratricidal contests, the invading forces

combine to struggle with those whose territory they
desire to plunder. Out of war springs alliance, the
alliance of armed and opposing powers. Large alliances and wider conflicts are made and begun. Struggle
develops special powers, which, continued and perfected through generations, become inheritances.

Man himself has such a history and such an origin.
He hates the rival claimants for the food which he
requires. He loathes his loneliness. He finds a mate
in whose ear he can breathe his detestation of the
horrible world, and breathe too his hope of ease after
conflict. He for her, she for him, the partners labour
for each other: a family, a group of families grow up,
and become at once an organised selfishness and a
society. Tribes, states, wide confederacies are established upon the same double foundation, of alliance
between the members and hostility to all who are not
members of the group. A silence falls, a stillness in
the conflict, and in the faces of opponents men see
a likeness to their own, in the faces of their kindred
the evidence of difference and hostility—and the old
barriers break, man sickens in loneliness again; but
revives once more, and guesses at a larger unity: the
world shall be his home, he declares, and all men his
brothers. He guesses at a more sublime unity; he
guesses at God, whose presence has always haunted
him; the forebodings and alarms, the hopes and as-
pirations of his earlier life, suggested by mere events,
manifestations of this or that several force, combine
in his memory, and now seem to be the varied operations not of many separate powers, but of one. With

that one he claims alliance, against that one he measures his pitiful strength, into that one he is taken up. His world, which is himself, is become one with God, who, because self-love is intolerable, breaks himself into that manifold which we call the world once more, and proves divinity articulate by entering into the form of every living thing.

CHAPTER XIII

ARTISTS AND MEN

LET us imagine ourselves in any company of people at liberty to ask each one whether he is a plain man or an artist. What will be the answer? One will reply "An artist? indeed not!" And there will be a note of indignation in his voice. Another will laugh and proclaim himself a plain man, showing how odd he thought the inquiry. Others will say that the question is not necessary: "Surely you can see for yourself"—and so indeed we can. They are plain men. Not artists, but plain men—that will be the reply we shall get from almost all—from ninety-nine out of a hundred. But when we agree with them quickly, heartily, and with an air of unhesitating acceptance, and look once more into their faces we shall surprise a sharp but courageously veiled disappointment. Let us look once more into those faces and we shall learn that something more is to be said, and perhaps will be said—"Plain, yes; but—but, I beg you believe, not so plain as I appear"—"plain no doubt, but not so plain as the next man or the last." "Plain, but mark you, with a distinction." "I am exactly like my neighbour, or the people of my class; only I have managed to come nearer than they to our common ideal."

The word is out—let us forget it for a moment. A gentleman must drawl and drop his g's and some

of his h's, precisely as another gentleman affects these
habits; but each is aware of a certain special propriety in his own use of a custom. A lady must be
in the fashion, and may even employ the same dress-
maker as some other (to be sure, the best) ladies, and
that devoted and skilful woman will do her utmost
for all her clients. Since each one of them would
blush to wear the wrong thing, we may take it that
each is wearing the right thing; why then is each
conscious of superiority? It is because she knows how
to put on and carry the uniform, the livery of the
fashion. For a fashion is like a faith, a thing delivered
to us by authority, to be accepted and yet to be interpreted; and orthodoxy is driven to criticism for fear
of being overtaken by dulness.

Yet a fashion is not Fashion, a faith is not Faith:
there are fashions and fashions, faiths and faiths; a
man who is an adherent, perhaps even an exemplary
adherent of this mode or that creed may reasonably
declare that he cannot at the same time adopt a mode
or a creed which is different from his own; but he
cannot reasonably deny that his neighbour who is an
adherent, perhaps also an exemplary adherent of that
other mode, that rival creed, is a man of Fashion, a
man of Faith. Men express their loyalty to Faith
and Fashion as best they may in the varying and
temporary forms of this mode and this creed, or of
that other mode and that other creed. Expression
they need, for without it they cannot be understood
by themselves or by their fellows; but in every utterance they define not only themselves but also Faith

and Fashion, those majestic and infinite powers.
Pearl buttons mark correctness upon the trouser leg
of a coster-monger, but a solicitor eschews them.
A silk hat was and, so it is rumoured, is again to be
worn by persons who shall do the right thing—but
what is right depends on time and place. The strictest
of men will refuse—justly refuse—to wear it on the
river, though they will cling to it at a wedding or at
a funeral or in the hunting-field. Yet there are trustworthy pictures of bearded youths wearing this head-
dress in racing boats on the Thames. Strange fellows
we think they look in those faded prints; stranger
still should we think them if they came to life, and
struck the familiar waters with their oars. But in
their own day, they were just plain men. Or we may
well believe, if there was anything to remark about
them, it was that they were plainer than the plain.
They lifted plainness to a certain elevation. There
is a distinction for a man in being more orthodox than
other members of his party or persuasion. This is not
vulgarity, but it is near it; it is almost heroic.

And yet we must remark that these instances are
of things common to a class, a section; not common
to humanity. For after all, a man may be a man
without being a costermonger; and if a costermonger,
richly dight with pearl buttons, he may fall short of
the most rigorous and the widest demands of humanity. Indeed we all fall short of those demands,
and the best that we can hope for in ourselves is a
devoted service of the fashion which governs our
region, our quarter or our class. To that we must

truly belong, and anything that shall signalise us must be a special completeness and perfection of our fitness to our station. To adapt ourselves to our environment without losing our individuality is the problem in which we are all engaged. How much store we set on solving it! and how many and how costly are our mistakes! We hate to be singular, but we should hate not less to be passed by! A respectable person, if we may take the word at its face value, is a person at whom people turn back to look once again: his ordinariness simply glistens. And it glistens because it is diligently polished.

Polishing, as we know, wears down some substances and makes them very thin. Life wears away our roughnesses, our angles, our excrescences and oddities, and we are delighted to have grown like our neighbours; but we may presently be worn to shadows and at last to mere nothingness, invisible before we are quite dead—yet loyal throughout to our hope and faithful to our pattern. How lucky if the pattern was a decent thing indeed, and really fit for us. But to be pressed into a form for which we were wholly unfitted, or into a form unworthy even of us, and to rejoice in our sufferings—to try to identify our faith with Faith, our fashion with Fashion—that were a parody of heroism meet for the tears of angels. Addison gives an account of a "young man of very lively parts, and of a sprightly turn in conversation, who had only one fault, which was an inordinate desire of appearing fashionable." Of the desire to be like the members of his class no complaint is made;

it is the urgency, the extravagance, the inordinacy of
his desire that is noted:

> This ran him into many amours, and consequently into
> many distempers. He never went to bed until two o'clock
> in the morning, because he would not be a queer fellow;
> and was every now and then knocked down by a constable
> to signalise his vivacity. He was initiated into half a
> dozen clubs before he was one and twenty; and so im-
> proved in them his natural gaiety of temper, that you
> might frequently trace him to his lodgings by a range of
> broken windows, and other the like monuments of wit
> and gallantry. To be short, after having fully established
> his reputation of being a very agreeable rake, he died of
> old age at five and twenty[1].

He was a martyr to plainness; his world was that
of a certain fashion and he desired to play a full part
in it; to do less than that, he felt, would be to make
himself singular and exceptional. Yet one cannot but
feel that the very success of his efforts to avoid peculiarity marked him out from his crowd. He became
plainer than the plain, he was more thorough-going
than the rest in very mediocrity. The mean which he
hit was indeed an extreme. He was drawn to the
centre of his special world as to the vortex of a whirl-
pool and untimely drowned in it, and making himself
pitiable made his little universe ridiculous.

Most men desiring to achieve a round measure of
plainness explore the boundaries of their world: they
are cast up by a tumultuous wave, or by a temerarious
stroke lift themselves to the edge of a new country.
To be sure they do not describe their own fortunes

---

[1] *Spectator*, No. 576.

in this language; they do not think about them in
this way. They would rather tell us if they were able
to tell us the truth, that they were at once devotees
and critics of the conventions which they admired;
that they sought and found a point of vantage from
which they could survey them. But what risks they
run! The detachment which they enjoy as critics
they may be condemned to endure as exiles; they
may not be able to get back to their native element.
The temper of devotion to their antique custom may
unfit them to appreciate a new mode of life. If the
specialist is a suicide the man of the world may pay
for his wide travels the price of homelessness.

We cherish peculiarity but hate to be considered
eccentric. Let us imagine ourselves introduced to a
stranger but provided only with the information that
he is an artist. Let us presume for the convenience
of our argument that he is as yet not widely known
to fame; or, if that is unfair, and if all artists are
famous, let us suppose that we have missed most un-
luckily the reverberating echoes of his renown. "You
are an artist, Sir?" we enquire, distrusting ourselves,
and hoping that he will give us the help we need for
drawing our conversation to a decent length; and
what is his reply? "I paint" or "I play the violin,"
and his statement is as short and sharp as if he had
said "an artist, yes I make chimney-pots" or "I sell
cheese." If we take him at his word, he will show at
once that he is affronted; he lets us see that we have
done him an injury. He claims to be a man among
men, a citizen of the same world as the rest of us, but

dealing with that world, interpreting it to himself and himself to it through the medium of his special business or art; he will have us accept him as for most purposes a plain man, and the truth may very well be that he is as plain as he professes himself. An artist must pay his rent and may even pay his tailor. An artist, though perhaps not every artist, has been known to drive a hard bargain, to make a good investment and build up a solid balance with his bankers; and a man who is known or desires to be known to the world as a painter or as a musician cannot but be known to his own family and to his own servants as one who plays other than his professional parts.

The artist is tempted to make two mistakes: first, to persuade himself that the point of view which he has adopted is the only point of view, and second, to believe that his rendering of the world as he apprehends it from his position is the world itself. When he makes the first mistake, he becomes an egotist and a propagandist; when he makes the second he too falls into a sorry materialism. The egotist is a man so much delighted with himself that he stereotypes himself, and, as it were, prints off as many copies as he can to be distributed like tracts in an ungrateful though perhaps a patient world.

Art is a way of doing things; the art of painting is the way, a way, this man's, that man's way of painting; the art of screw-making is the way, a way of making screws; there is also an art of getting on. Now by the time a man has found out a way of doing anything, and brought it to near perfection, he has got a certain facility in doing that thing; he goes on doing it, and prides himself on his dexterity. It is easier for him to do that than to do other things, it is almost easier for him to do that than to do nothing. He does at length by a mental machinery what at first cost him the pain of thought and tired hands. He becomes a factory; perhaps he builds a factory. It is all one. He has a recognised style; his pictures are known, they can be recognised; his screws command the market; his poems are the rage; his pills are a household word and perhaps a people's medicine, good for all ailments, to be taken on land and sea; or he is a wit, a licensed wit, and repeats himself and is repeated. It is his way of doing what he has learnt to do and his facility has become a formula.

Whatever we do we are dealing with the world, focussing it for ourselves, ferreting our way into it, boring it with our painters' eyes or our screws, burying ourselves in the rut which we have made. We see as much as we give ourselves the chance of seeing; and the danger of success is that we strive to maintain for ever a pose which we have once taken and found pleasing or useful. Was there ever a girl who caught herself at a glass or mirrored in an affectionate eye, who was loath to repeat the gesture, to renew the winning attitude? Was there ever a man who, having said a good thing, sternly denied himself the joy of saying it again? But the repetition may be made too often; and the art, the pretty way of doing the thing, the happy *mot*, may become a trick. A trick is art debased; a trick is art looking at itself, and courting by deliberate coyness or meretricious cleverness, the plaudits of a world which has learned to clap its hands and forgotten how to smile.

Yet we need not banish the familiar; we may allow a conservatism, an economy in jests; we may confess our love of hearing the old stories of our friends, and of telling again and again our own. Such sentiments are common and right. Familiarity itself may give a new wealth, may bestow a fresh charm upon a thing prized, and drawn from the treasure of memory to grace a recurrent festival.

We are all artists at heart; or are we playing tricks? A mite may be convinced that all the world is a cheese; but if it attacks the cheese which is its world with vigour, driving ever new avenues through it, riddling it, consuming it, and perishing at last tired out with its own versatility, it would be a broad-minded mite. Or a man who has failed in a hundred attempts to write or paint or dance or make money, may essay one more adventure and still one more, baffled but not daunted, and drawing from the variety of his defeated but ever renewed efforts an unfailing interest in the world which mocks and provokes him. It concerns him, that world; he cannot let it be; and it will not let him be, though it may almost starve him. Such a man is more conversant with the world than another who has hit home, thrust in, and made his way straight to success. The one is alive; the other dead.

The artist may make the mistake of supposing that

what he sees is the whole world—but he pays the
penalty; he ceases to be an artist. It is his prero-
gative, since he is human, to take a point of view;
if he is absorbed in himself, if he identifies what he
sees with all that might be seen, he perishes. He
becomes a monument of mere achievement. To live
he must move; and to move is to see new and
different worlds.

The plain man often has a wider range than the
professed artist. Not enamoured by his own phrases,
not enchanted by the view afforded him by the windows
of his office, he may take a rare holiday and see the big
world at work or at play, and return to his desk with
eyes enriched and illumined, more broadly and pro-
foundly educated than that other who spends his life
seizing one landscape or one face or one type of
landscape and face, and imprisoning it and his own
soul on a saleable or even an unsaleable canvas.

The plain man often has a much wider, a more
liberal training than the scholar: the world is his
University; even if he makes cheeses he studies the
palates and the purses of those who are to buy and
eat them. It is good for an artist to have his price;
but not good for him to be precious. He must learn
to sell his works, and keep himself inviolate. He
should take a lesson from the market-place. Even
the advertisements of trade have a large impersonal-
ity. Mr Rowland was no doubt a man; but we
think of him as a hair-restorer. Mr Pears gives or
gave us soap and withheld himself, and asked us for
nothing but our shillings, knowing that we would give

them if we could give our approval with them. The
artist claims and begs for our allegiance; but should
accept it only if we keep for ourselves a proud inde-
pendence. His work he puts on the market; himself
he offers us as a gift; and we cannot possess the work,
however much we may have paid for it, unless we
take the gift, freely indeed, yet at the high cost of
understanding him. He has the self-abandonment of
true pride, and wrapt in a splendid nakedness defies
our curiosity and disregards our stare. He throws the
passion of a life into the ecstasy of a moment; he
gives the toilsome practice of years to a work on
which we may bestow a hurried glance—it is enough
that he has done what he could for that, and he goes
on to do what next awaits him. Is immortality his
reward? Yes; but at the price of death renewed; for
every reader or spectator he is born afresh; and with
each he dies. He transcends himself; and escapes
through the asceticism of love to the fulfilment of
desire; he is forgotten but lives.

CHAPTER XIV

THE TEACHER'S ART

" ART" and "artist" are words which we are apt to confine within limits too narrow. Art is, we have maintained, a way of doing a thing, but it is more than that: it is an excellent way of doing a thing, and excellence is not achieved without devotion and practice. The artist is a man who has won or is diligently pursuing excellence. But he must be content to forsake much that seems good to himself and to other men, if he is to reach this goal.

The world is spread before the artist as it is spread before any other man; he cannot but see it; he hears the voices with which it speaks to him and to other men; it reaches out to him and touches him. With it he must have dealings, with it he must maintain a conversation; he must eat and drink, and sleep and wake; he must have clothes and a house; but he tries either to hasten through his other business with the world as quickly as he can in order to have leisure for what he calls his work, or else he tries to make all his other business contribute to his main interest and serve his dominant ambition. The world has seldom applauded his judgment; it has found fault with him either for giving scanty attention to matters which in dignity and in importance, in usefulness and in consideration seemed to it to outweigh the one thing to which the artist hastened to betake himself, or for striving to subordinate serious concerns to play.

We may grant that, if the artist's play is of a kind that can afford amusement to the onlooker, the world has been ready to look on; if in his play he showed an agility, a skill marvellous to the beholder, it rewarded him with the gaze of wondering eyes, and regarded him as a spectacle; but the artist remained a "player," and the exhibition which he provided was a "show." These names for himself and for his performance the artist has not been unwilling to adopt, and has confirmed the world in its opinion that the man and what he does are not serious, and scarcely real. And then, he is making an exhibition of himself, and this the world of plain men believes itself very loath to do. There may indeed be an artist, here and there, one out of many, a rare creature who can sell his wares at a figure which catches the eye of the plain man, and makes him wonder whether after all the artist is the fool he once seemed to be; but quickly he corrects himself for the trouble of having had to think twice by declaring that not at any price would he make an exhibition of himself or do in public what the artist does.

No, the plain man will not make an exhibition of himself, though his name stands in large letters of advertisement set thickly in every town and strewn freely in country villages and beside the railroads. He is not disposed to regard himself as a candidate for notoriety—at any rate, not for notoriety of that sort. The artist is, in his language, an entertainer,

and though he may flatter himself that he is indeed
entertaining, he would shrink with horror from the
suggestion of becoming a public entertainer. Great
names he might use in support of this sentiment.
Aristotle, here at one with Plato, expressed it for the
Greeks. A citizen, a ruler, might permit himself to
enjoy the performances of a professional entertainer,
a musician or a dancer, but himself would not desire
to rival them. There are some arts which a man may
practise in moderation and as an amateur; but he
should blush to have more than an amateur's skill in
them, or to go beyond the reputable bounds of
moderation. Latin literature, and not only with the
pens of Satirists, bears witness to the recognition of
this convention in Rome and the Roman world. In
England we know that it is or has been held unseemly
to have more than a gentleman's or a lady's proficiency in arts which are and always were held in
honour. Even in our games we distinguish between
"gentlemen" and "players," and here we find once
more the notion of play identified with the notion of
professionalism. The profession of the arts, especially
perhaps of the arts of painting and of music, has been
characteristic of "Bohemia," and though visits to
that vaguely defined· territory may be a permissible
and pardonable diversion for persons who could not
by any mistake be conceived to be natives or even
naturalised dwellers in it, the visits, it is generally
agreed, must not be too frequent or too long. The
emphasis, the value which Bohemians set upon things
may provoke a tolerant smile or even a generous laugh,

but it is the impropriety of the emphasis, the dispro-
portion of the value which afford us, who are not
Bohemians, our merriment. And nothing probably
marks the difference between Bohemians and the
polite world more decisively than the affectation of
Bohemianism by persons who have as little claim to
be artists as they have to be staunch defenders of the
established, though sometimes endangered, conventions upheld by correct and unintelligent patrons of
the arts.

The artist, for good or for ill, with well directed
choice or with lamentable error, has said for himself
"This one thing I do." And the ultimate question
to be asked about him is whether his declaration is
to be accepted literally or not. If the answer is that
he is engaged literally in one thing, then in seeking
to save his soul he has lost it. But if the one thing
which he does is the medium, the language, in which
he speaks to the large and general world, if it is the
language through which he interprets whatever the
world has to say to him, then in losing his life he has
gained it. Abandoning himself in his work, he has
acquired the supreme art of conversation with the
world, he has a passport into it because he can contribute to its welfare and make it contribute to his own.

A sensible man will not refuse to listen to what
other men say upon themes in regard to which he can
only be a listener, but he will listen in the hope of
presently seizing a meaning which now escapes him,
and, by translating it, of widening the range at once
of his language and of his experience. He will not

deign to speak of the whole of his experience, for he
knows the difference between discourse and unlicensed
and unregulated chatter. He selects from his experience those parts which are especially significant,
the parts namely in which he has made some sharp
and memorable discovery of himself, or in which he
believes that he has surprised in sudden revela-
tion or after patient search found the meaning
of his own heart, and made his own experience intelligible to himself. These elements selected, he
orders and arranges with a double purpose: he wishes
to get them quite clear and distinct; he wishes also
to bring them into the coherence of a living system,
to articulate them, to give them free and concerted
movement. But he does not forget that a living
system maintains itself not only by the fine poise of
its parts, but by the relationship which it also establishes and enlarges with other systems and with the
general world. The result is that for him self-realisation brings a keen and sensitive consciousness of the
reality of other people.

The artist is notorious for his self-consciousness; it
may become morbid; it cannot indeed become too
delicate, for the finest delicacy goes with health and
strength: but it will save him from shouldering a
clumsy way through the world, and if it renders him
quick to receive and to enjoy kindness, the delightful
recognition of kinship, where kinship exists and kindness is its natural expression, it may arm him against
unkindness by teaching him, after many sorrows endured, that where no kinship is there is in fact no

relationship; and without relationship there is no reality. If it is true that till he has learnt this lesson he will pay for his sensibility with pain, it is not less true that till he has learnt it his sensibility falls something short of perfection. "This one thing I do" is a claim which we expect from the religious man; but it is now clear that this is because the religious man is an artist. His art is life; he has his way; his life and his way are also truth. There is no greater claim that a man can make; there is none smaller that is worth a man. For this claim reconciles the personal with the universal, emotion with reason; it is the claim of a man who being able to discourse with himself offers his heart with a bold reserve to the world and wrests its heart in requital for his own.

The teacher being human can make no other claim than this. Yet he may run a special risk of being misunderstood. We must assume that the teacher has the rigour of conscience and the eagerness of inquiry, which mark the scholarly temper. He may have and cultivate this temper even if he has no great wealth of learning, and without this temper learning is mere baggage carried by a beast of burden walking with uncertain steps upon two legs, a sorry substitute for the sure-footed ass. Learned or not, the teacher-scholar is a man who is bent upon doing one thing. The one thing which he has to do is to quicken for himself the reality of his subject, and to persuade the world of its reality. He exposes himself to attack from two quarters at once; we arraign him as a fanatic and as a tyrant. Fanatic we call him because he must

look at the world from his own standpoint, and tyrant
because he is fain to compel us others to look at it
from the same position. How many angels may set
their celestial feet upon a needle's point is a fertile
if an unanswerable question; how many men can
share with another his standpoint is a question to
which the summary answer is "None." A greengrocer
driving his wholesome trade may supply his customers with greens, but he may not force them to
buy: and if long and affectionate contemplation of
the produce of the vegetable garden has screened his
very mind with a cabbage-coloured veil he has no
right to fasten however thin a gauze of green upon
our eyes. Yet if he speaks to us and tries for our
understanding to paint what he sees he cannot be
honest if he stubbornly refuses to employ that very
pigment which renders the dominant hue of his world.
If he attempted honesty at this price he could achieve
only colourlessness, and that would be meaningless-
ness.

The teacher is more subtly tempted than the greengrocer to become a tyrant. Those of us, indeed, who
pay his bill, and in that sense are his customers, are his
contemporaries and may be strong to withstand him:
but those who receive what he has to give are younger
and less well practised in self-defence: for them, soft
and untried, his persuasion has the force of authority,
and when they do not know what he means they may
deceive him and themselves by repeating what he
has said as if they meant it. And if he is satisfied that
what he says is the truth, if he is assured even that

he provides not indeed all that his pupils need but
a part of what they need for the fulfilment of their
own lives and the discharge of their duties in the
world, for carrying on their conversation with it,
then it is easy for him to mistake the facile repetition
of his doctrine for its interpretation.

Yet now, when he stands on the edge of sheer disaster, his fanaticism may save him, for the fanatic
has quick ears for heresy, and catching the note of
mimicry or missing the accent of conviction quickly
determines that to be a tyrant is to be both an im-
postor and a dupe. He will not suffer the object of
his devotion to be profaned. He may find delight in
mathematics or in classics or in whatever subject; he
may work hard to convey some knowledge to his
pupils; he may try to quicken and foster in them
some genuine appreciation of it; he may hope that
they too will find delight in it; but he will not expect
that their appreciation or their delight will be his own;
for he knows that they are and will always be themselves and is resolved to remain himself. His standpoint they cannot take, and he would not have them
take it. Being an artist he is condemned to a divine
loneliness; their ways are not his ways, nor their
thoughts his thoughts.

But his loneliness wakes in him, as in a god, the
energy of creation, and he makes as best he can
a world with which he speaks; to a void he brings
substance, to chaos order, he arranges and disposes,
and bestows the gift of speech; conversation he must
have with his pupils; and they must become articu-

late, and then the language which he and they hold together is the language of partial understanding clouded by apprehension, cleared by reconciliation, silenced by estrangement, and renewed by atonement ever to be renewed, a sacrifice in which his life is spent. At the end he is solitary still, but he has discovered himself; he may have helped his pupils to discover themselves; they may, pupils and teacher, find and behold the "subject" with which so long they had been wrestling, they in the dark and he in something less than daylight, illumined as by a shaft from a heavenly dawn.

This is the best recompense that a teacher may aspire to get, this brightening of his own vision, this assurance that his pupils have seen, not what he sees, but something which has kindled in their eyes the gleam of recognition. Yet the teacher is a plain man too; he remembers that the little world of his own creation is set in another, larger world; in it his pupils and he move, and soon they move apart. He indeed cannot travel far from his base, his centre, his classroom, his shop, and when he travels it is a long path which his own going and coming have beaten hard; they will range more widely. Only for a short time he has their society. Like as the leaves, so are the generations of men. Faster than the generations of men, pupils come and go. It is not with them only that he has to deal. It is also with that larger world, that void, that chaos from which he seemed to call them, that strange and alien society into which they depart—it is with that world that he must converse and do his business. He sells his goods, such as may be bought; he commands his price, the best he can afford time and trouble to bargain for; and some time and some trouble he must devote to bargaining; but himself he gives without price to those who can take him; yet always upon the condition, which not all the world can understand, that he never gives himself away.

CHAPTER XV

IMPRISONMENT AND FREEDOM

WE have called Education the process by which men acquire the art of conversation, the practice of pleasant and useful intercourse with their fellows. It is clear that men can never have wholly lacked this art, never been wholly unversed in this practice. For convenience, and in order to support theories to which they were for good or bad reasons pledged, certain great writers have indeed drawn imaginary pictures of human life as they have feigned that it was conducted before society was formed; but, though these pictures have had and still retain a value, it is agreed that they are imaginary, and that well or ill their authors have been feigning. History can tell us nothing of men apart from society. At the very dawn of the world men found themselves in a society, the reality of which they wished at once to prove and to strengthen; they discovered themselves engaged in commerce with this society, and since they longed to quicken and multiply their relationships with it, they determined that they must first understand its nature.

In the demand insistently made at the present day for education, for more education, and for education of an increasing number of persons, we have an endorsement, a confirmation of the account which we have given of Education. For the plain and potent reason which has made people ask for education is that they have felt with distress that they had not fully acquired or perfectly mastered the art of conversation, the practice of pleasant and useful intercourse with their fellows. On some matters they have, it is true, learned to converse, on some they are able to maintain intercourse with their fellows; but even upon these they have been conscious that by a clumsiness in their use of speech, by a bluntness in their modes of thought they have been kept from a full understanding even of those persons with whom they have held a halting conversation and from drawing the full benefit which the matters which they have handled would have yielded to a finer touch. And they have been conscious, moreover, that they have been debarred from approach to other matters, the objects of their longing, of their jealous, if unintelligent regard. Some persons, they have been aware, can deal deftly with the matters with which they themselves are roughly familiar, and have easy access to and command of other matters which they themselves cannot reach. They are disposed to envy these more fortunate or better equipped persons both for having a special mastery of the world which they themselves know with that rough familiarity, and for holding the secret of another world which they do not know. Into that other world they desire to enter.

Here they make a distinction between society and the best society. The charge of snobbery is easily made and may be lightly repelled. The truth is that every man makes the distinction between the best and whatever falls short of excellence, even if his only criterion of the "best" is the cold and desolating fact that he is himself excluded from it. He perceives that those people who have the best are strong in their purpose to keep it and to vindicate for their children an inheritance in it; and if he cannot entertain the hope of getting it for himself, he will not abandon the hope of winning it for his children. The desire for education is a desire to keep or to get a place in the great society of men. It may lead a man astray; he may be attracted rather by what shows and glitters than by what is real and recondite, rather by the temporal than by the eternal. But it is a desire which may be purified and ennobled, even by the trial of disappointment and of long waiting.

Some very hard problems have to be faced and conquered before we can expect to attain a truly educated society. Such a society must be made up of members who can converse about those things which are necessary for their life and for the maintenance of the society which they form. What are those necessary things? They are food and housing and clothing and exercise for the body; all these must be provided; but they are also an equipment for the mind, a housing of the spirit. Now the needs of the body have not in fact been provided except by the toil of multitudes, who when this toil is done have little strength and little time for furnishing their minds, their spirits; and this toil has hitherto only brought its results because those persons who have given to it the labour of their hands have been guided

and controlled by other persons who being largely
or wholly free from such labour, have been free to
devote themselves to the tasks of direction and of
management.

It may be indeed that directors and managers are
not, all of them, conspicuously marked by ability for
their office; but with such success as they have
achieved, little or great, they have discharged it, and
they will not without a struggle allow themselves to
be dislodged. They are not anxious to change places
with those others. And if they should be suddenly
and violently removed from the places which they
now hold, it is certain that for a time the world would
move less easily, less comfortably; for if the directors
and managers have as little native ability as their
envious detractors allow them, they have the advantage of experience; they have learned by experience how to do what they have been in the habit
of doing. But if we ask why they are determined to
keep their places the answer is quick to come: it is
because they agree that these places are more to be
desired than the others, and not only because they
afford more food and clothing and housing and all
these of a superior quality, but because in addition
to all these advantages they afford power, security,
leisure. Power may be grossly and cruelly used:
security may bring on a mental and moral obesity;
leisure, ill spent, may ill deserve the name; but leisure,
security, power, men desire and pursue.

There is a bitter kernel of truth in what Phocylides
says, "that when one has got enough to live on, one

should practise excellence[1]." A carpenter has a work
to do, and if he should be prevented, by illness for
example, from doing it, he might say that life for
him would not be worth living; but he might also say
that unless he could go on with his work he could
not live. As Professor Bosanquet remarks in his
short but lucid note on this passage, "Excellence, for
Plato, means doing something well[2]." The excellence
which a carpenter can achieve is that of doing a
carpenter's work well, of proving himself, by the
quality of his work, an excellent carpenter. But,
when he has done this, he may have little or nothing
left of time and of energy for doing anything else
well, for achieving excellence in any other activity;
and if he seeks leisure, however nobly he may hope
to employ it, at the price and on the condition of
neglecting his carpentering, he will lose, with his
trade, his livelihood. What then is he to do, if while
he plies his trade or, in such few and hard won
moments of repose as he can win from it, he uneasily
guesses at excellence of another kind, and allows himself in pardonable day-dreams the hope of achieving
it by fulfilling the function of a carpenter and some
other function *in addition*? Is he to quench the hope;
is he to put away his dreams? And what are we, the
other members of the society to which he belongs
and in which he plays his necessary part, to say to
him? Dare we make use of "one splendid falsehood[3],"

[1] Plato, *Rep.* III 407 A.
[2] *Education of the Young in the* Republic *of Plato*, p. 113.
[3] Plato, *Rep.* III, 414 B.

selecting it from those other "convenient falsehoods" with which we try to maintain the arrangement of society in orders, grades, professions, trades, to which we have grown accustomed?

We may proclaim the dignity of labour, and acknowledge that for every order in our society there is an appropriate work, which its members must do; we may with Plato believe that justice, that central and unifying principle which holds society together, is nothing but "every man's minding his own business"; but we shall still have to say that one business, one work is not another, and one is higher than another in a scale of values which we with difficulty define but which we with conviction adopt. Even for a man whose business or work is higher than that of the rest, the question may arise, sharp as a sword, whether he is fit for his high task. This is a question which a man's neighbours may be more ready to ask in clear words than he is himself; though a man of finely disciplined and sensitive nature may ask it, in silence, of himself. For other men whose labour is done upon a lower plane the question may be whether their work is fit and good enough for them. This is a question which they may be more ready to ask for themselves than other men for them; though here again men of finely disciplined and sensitive nature may not think of asking it, or refuse to ask it if it occurs to them, for themselves; yet other men, whose work is of a different sort, may sometimes ask it on their behalf and for the sake of society.

Are we to pretend or can we constrain ourselves

to believe that the carpenter is a carpenter *by nature*, the soldier a soldier *by nature*, and the man who belongs to what till yesterday was called the governing class, *by nature* a governor? Shall we tell over again the "Phoenician tale" and say to our fellow citizens

All of you in the state are brothers; but God in fashioning you mingled gold in the creation of as many as are fit to be rulers; and silver, in the auxiliaries; and iron and brass in the husbandmen and other artificers[1].

Can we be quite sure of the ingredients; are we satisfied that it was God who mingled them in the composition of men according to their several orders in the state? Certainly this is a story for which we shall find it hard to win belief; we may hesitate, as Socrates hesitated, to tell it. But it is only a part of the story; an earlier part, at once simpler and subtler, we have passed over and must now recall. We shall tell

first the rulers themselves, and the soldiers and next the rest of the community as well that all the time we were nurturing and educating them, it was so to speak a dream in which they thought that all this befell them and was done to them; but in reality they were themselves being fashioned and nurtured in the earth beneath, and their arms and the rest of their array were being wrought[2].

Whatever "nature" may have done, here we have the open confession that nurture and education have done not less to make men what they are, and by making them what they are to place and fix them in the order in which they now find themselves. Nurture and education have preceded their real birth; it was only, "when they were completely finished, that the

[1] Plato, *Rep.* 414 C, D.   [2] *Op. cit.* 415 A.

earth who was their mother sent them forth." How shall we persuade men to believe all this? We cannot hope to persuade those to whom we tell the story, fresh and incredible, for the first time. Yet, if it is repeated over and over, their children and their children's children may learn to accept it, or at least not to question it. The long years in their course may leave upon men the deposit of a tradition, which shall first be a covering and then an overgrowth and at last fasten itself into the very fibre and living tissue of their minds.

But what time has wrought time can undo; a day comes when men are forced upon self-analysis by the anomalies of the world which they see; they unravel the web of conventions; they disengage their minds from inveterate beliefs, they break the spell of tradition. Perceiving in a sudden and shocking discovery the poverty of their lot, the narrowness of the paths in which they have been wont to travel to and fro, the sharp limits of their careers, they make the announcement, some timidly for their own ears and some so that the world may hear, that they are by nature other and more than practitioners of their craft, their profession, their calling however high or low it may be in the social order. They claim to be men[1], to live with their peers and to converse with them. If in a spirit of brotherhood, proud and generous, they greet all men as peers and attempt to speak an equal and intelligible language with them, they find themselves at once at grips again with that riddle to which the tradition so painfully and so triumphantly over-

[1] Cf. Aristotle, *Eth. Nic.* I. 7.

thrown was lately the customary, the unchallenged answer.

What is the world in which their new, large conversation is to be held, what is to be their universe of discourse? It is a world, or universe, of which each one of them is himself the centre; each one has or is his own world, his own universe. The circle in which he dwells and about the horizon of which his hungry eye roves is cut indeed by many other circles; but even if the centre of any one of these should fall within the circumference of his own he cannot take his stand upon it: it is held impregnably by another man, and for himself he must stay, a prisoner after all, upon the centre of *his* circle. And with many circles he can share only a little segment of common ground; the greater part of most of them must lie outside and beyond his boundaries. He may be tempted to imagine that, as of those worlds of which he sees parts there are other parts withheld from his scrutiny, so yet further again in a vaster world, in a universe not of "*his* discourse" at all, there are spheres not undreamed but certainly unknown. But who shall say of any man that there are not worlds of which he does not even dream? Yet from worlds not his own but bordering on and overlapping his own he draws some things which he needs or desires; to them he contributes what he can or yields what is by force taken from him.

He is fain to solve his problem, and can think of nothing better than the old solution that society is brought into being by the stark but reconciling fact that no man is self-sufficing. He needs what others have; he must give what others claim. Loneliness hits him hard; he stretches out his hand to other lonely men. But it must not be an empty hand: something he must have to offer, the produce of his labour spent upon his domain, some gift of his own nature cultivated within the confines which hem it in; and, if labour is to be thus bestowed and nature so cultivated, then every man is once more a craftsman, every man has his own profession, is set in an order, a rank once more. Co-operation involves division of work, and what division more just than that which matches aptitude? Or, if the division be unjust, if the allotment of functions is made by chance and corresponds ill or not at all to varieties of nature, then use will tame nature and make it subservient to a new tradition which the more easily takes the place of the old because it is almost exactly like it.

No man has time, no man is well enough off, to reach "excellence" save in that one thing to which he devotes himself or is by necessity bound.

The wisdom of a learned man cometh by opportunity of leisure; and he that hath little business shall become wise. How can he get wisdom that holdeth the plough, and that glorieth in the goad, that driveth oxen, and is occupied in their labours, and whose talk is of bullocks? [1]

The opportunity of leisure may not be properly prized and turned to fruitful use; but without leisure, wisdom, if Ecclesiasticus is to be trusted, cannot be had; a man may have little business and still be a

[1] Ecclesiasticus xxxviii, 24, 25.

fool; yet a man who will not keep his mind free and at peace, who will not stoutly refuse to be for ever busy, will never become wise. A man who has little business may indeed fill part of his leisure with the contemplation of poverty, as a close neighbour or even a partner of his life; he will not embrace wealth, which rarely consorts with leisure, for it is produced by busy men and makes busy men busier still.

The wise man may not desire wealth; but what if he desires knowledge of the ways of men? Can he get this knowledge if he spends his days and nights in meditation, and takes no part in the affairs of ordinary folk? Sometimes the recluse and solitary man may long to hold a plough, to urge the goad, to drive oxen; but he has no skill in these things; for he has been occupied in other labours. Is it his ambition to frame a theory of state, to plan a new society? or, as preliminary to these tasks, to analyse society as it is? How can he, without knowledge bought by experience of the real activities of real men in the world? Can he understand the world unless he will engage in its affairs? Let him betake himself to the country and he will soon learn that, though men whose "talk is of bullocks" have a small vocabulary, he cannot use it because he is either wholly ignorant of their business, or at any rate imperfectly acquainted with bullocks. If men who mind cattle have no leisure in which to get wisdom, he who seeks wisdom in leisure must forgo the experience of graziers.

Not less certainly must he forgo the special and proper experience of every other class of men. The carpenter and work-master, the jeweller and the smith and the potter—"all these trust to their hands and every one is wise in his work"—but not beyond his work. And the man of leisure cannot claim to be wise in the work of any one of them. If then we say that he may achieve "wisdom," his wisdom must evidently be of a different sort from the special, the specialised, wisdom of these other men. It must be general, it must be universal, it must be philosophic. Very few men can reach it; very few have qualities which entitle them to believe and to declare that leisure is their work. And they will be most keenly aware of the gulf which is fixed between them and other men. We need not say that they can never cross the gulf; but they are received as strangers upon its further bank, if indeed they are noticed at all, for it is by a flight of imagination that they come ghostly visitors, not seen, not felt by common sense, and the dwellers upon the other side having no wings cannot cross to the domain of leisured wisdom. Many of them may not know that there is such a domain; many may entertain for it the contempt which has its roots in the soil of ignorance ploughed by doubt; a few may stretch out yearning hands towards it. But all of them are fettered to their trades, and ply them as prisoners in separate cells.

They shall not dwell where they will, nor go up and down; they shall not be sought in public counsel nor sit high in the congregation: they shall not sit on the judges' seat, nor understand the sentence of judgment; they cannot declare justice and judgment, and they shall not be found where parables are spoken.

Yet "without these cannot a city be inhabited";

"they will maintain the state of the world, and their desire is in the work of their craft."

If the world is to be maintained in the state with which we are familiar or in any state, the work of the world must be done; the work is of many kinds and must be distributed among many kinds of men. Shall we refuse to divide men into "kinds"? Then we divide them into classes, into professions and trades. If work of any kind is to be done with the utmost efficiency and economy, then the people who do it must devote themselves to it; they can do little or nothing beside; their hands will be subdued to what they work in; their minds if not subdued will take something of the colour of their hands. It is not easy to say that there are not "kinds" of men: it is foolish to pretend that there is no danger of men's falling into different kinds. It is in fact the recognition of this danger which has armed us all in defence of what is sometimes called our common humanity. What men have hated for themselves and for their neighbours has been the doctrine, supported by strong evidence though not by the whole truth, that the carpenter is a carpenter and nothing more, the potter a potter and nothing more.

The carpenter's or the potter's work may be hard, it may long have been ill paid, and these conditions men may well try to escape or to improve; but it is not these conditions which have galled them and fed in them the fever of indignation or lit the fires of revolution. It is another condition, branded upon them by their neighbours or more terribly burned into their hearts by themselves, that to do the work of their trade, to exercise their craft, was to shut themselves into their trade or craft for ever and identify themselves with it. They longed to claim their share in a "common humanity." But what is this common humanity? It is a vast domain of which we may all profess ourselves the joint heirs, but it still needs tillage, and, though a man's eye may take in a wide expanse, he can but till that part of it on which he will settle and abide. His neighbours, his partners in humanity, are under the same necessity; they too must till the plot on which they are; and presently the plots become allotments, or gardens or orchards or fields fenced about and guarded by barriers of privilege, of ownership. Each plot will illustrate the individual qualities of the man who has worked it; each man in working it will have given, with expression, strength to his qualities, and will have taken some tincture of the soil which has local peculiarities showing through the general character of the whole domain.

He may lift his eyes and try again to survey his large inheritance; he may assure himself that the far horizon would yield to keener eyes and retreat if he travelled towards it; but what he will see will be the plots in which his neighbours have penned themselves with sharp-set hedges or solid walls against his too inquisitive regard, against his presumptuous approach. If thanks to increasing skill he has time left him, if his labour is done before night falls, he still cannot enjoy leisure: he puts down his tools, but his mind is still in his furrows. What goes on behind the ramparts where his neighbours, those partners in a common humanity, have established themselves, he may ask, but he cannot know; is he to guess that they are like himself; that they are slaves of their trade; is he to suppose that they on their side sometimes wonder what he is doing and what manner of man he is? He may believe that he shares with them such imaginings, that they think, when their tale of work is finished day by day, of its relation to the work of other men and to his own, that they wonder how they and he make up a world, or try to figure to themselves the significance of "common humanity" in the terms of occupations, modes of life which they know too well, namely, their own, and in the terms which they can, of course, imperfectly use, of modes of life, occupations which they know too little, namely, those of other men.

If they dream these dreams, they may seem to themselves to reconquer a part of that inheritance from which the hard conditions of their life proclaim that they are banished. They are the richer and the poorer for these dreams: poorer because now a bitterness flavours their poverty as with gall; they confess themselves prisoners, but they suspect that they were born free, or at least that they sprang from no servile race; richer, because though prisoners still they look out from between their bars with eyes undimmed. They know that they are alive because they suffer pain, and would scorn to be eased, even if they might, of proof of their indomitable vitality.

CHAPTER XVI

SILENCE, MEDITATION AND PAIN

MR FREDERICK GREENWOOD in his very beautiful "Gospel of Content"[1] says that a prison is too good, and so unsuitable for common rogues and thieves: these

should give place to honest men—honest reflective men.... Imprisonment is wasted on persons of so inferior character. Waste it not, and you will have accommodation for wise men to learn the monk's lesson (did you ever think it all foolishness?) that a little imperious hardship, a time of seclusion with only themselves to talk to themselves, is most improving. For statesmen and reformers it should be an obligation.

It may be that if in solitude men will talk to themselves, and reflect upon the theme of their intimate discourse, they will find that they have done more than a little to make good their right to a common humanity, since silence, meditation, and pain are essential elements in it. The first fruits of emancipation are enjoyed with an ironic satisfaction by men who perceive that they are in prison. Others, who take the walls which incarcerate them for the utmost limits of the world, are by nature prisoners, prisoners in their souls; they need to be born again in order to learn that what they took for a universe is only a cage, through the bars of which they have not even been at the pains to look.

[1] *The Yellow Book*, vol. II, July 1894, p. 20.

If the popular demand for education were a demand for the opportunity to reflect, it would be of a nobler quality than it can now generally claim to be. Instead of that it is put forward with arguments for efficiency, for success, for getting on; and getting on means too often getting out of the class, the profession, the trade, in which a man's forbears were and in which he might not unnaturally remain, and getting into another class, or profession or trade to which he arrives *nouveau riche*, awkward or *blasé* or both. It is too rarely a demand to enter that world in which "parables" are spoken. We may look forward, if we choose to indulge our fancy, to a day when the progress of mechanical invention shall have enabled men to do in minutes what now they must take hours to do; but vacancy is not leisure and cannot yield wisdom; or we may forecast a day when mechanical invention shall have spent its energies, and when for sheer lack of the material of "civilisation"—coal, for instance, being exhausted—we shall hail the return of Nature with fields green once more and skies clear; yet Nature will prove herself a hard mistress and bind burdens upon men's backs which they will hardly bear.

Fancy may paint for us either picture, but not persuade us of its truth. For we are unable to plan a world in which men do not differ from each other, in which varying needs are not to be supplied by varying services, or varying services are not to be fulfilled by the exercise of varying gifts. Let us grant that any work which a man may do without loss of

self-respect he may do with honour; still we cannot
pretend that all kinds of work are of equal dignity;
there are some which in the doing and when they
are done afford more of that leisure in which wisdom
is garnered; such work any man may be pardoned
for making the goal of his ambition, but only if upon
a fair examination of himself he is satisfied that he
is indeed fit to undertake it. If he is satisfied, or if,
acknowledging his unfitness for it, he is yet urged
towards it by an imperious destiny which he cannot
withstand, then he can be more than pardoned; he
is justified. He made no vows; vows were made for
him. And, even so, the vows may receive a strange
fulfilment; he may travel a road that he never looked
to tread, and reaching the goal he may not recognise
it; or he may learn that the destiny which he believed
was pointing quite clearly to one goal was drawing
him to another. If moved by such influences a man
seeks to change his station, we may respect his purpose
even if we cannot approve his judgment.

But it is under the sway of very different influences
that many men attempt to make their way into a
profession, a mode of life, different from that of their
fathers. They see the outward conditions of leisure;
its meaning they do not see; they admire the tranquillity of the leisured man, they do not know the
"toil unsevered from tranquillity" which he accepts
as his portion. Thus many persons are attracted by
the conditions of life which the teacher and the
student appear to enjoy; and even if it is too late
for them to get these conditions for themselves they

strive to get them for their children. Even now there
is a certain social consideration granted in some
quarters to the student and the teacher; he earns his
perhaps scanty living without making his hands dirty,
and, though in a metaphor he may say that he
"sweats," there is a wonderful difference between the
language of metaphor and the language of plain facts;
and he has holidays. These are conditions which
seduce the ignorant and unwary. And then there is
an intellectual vulgarity, which tempts many persons
to prize knowledge for anything and for everything
except—itself. And there is a simpler vulgarity which
sets a high store on degrees which are sought as pretty
decorations are sought, and worn with the same
childish ostentation. That a degree represents a stage
of knowledge and equipment and training which a
man must pass before he enters upon the independent
study of any subject is even now not commonly con-
ceded.

Persons who make these mistakes cannot speak or
listen to the language of parables. No more can they
who, having passed beyond these mistakes or having
never made them, have yet become completely engrossed in one or another of the now almost innumerable special departments of science or of
learning. Parables have a local colour, but an infinite
significance. Men who use parables exhibit at their
highest development the qualities specially characteristic of their calling, but interpreting them in a
free translation then carry them beyond the confines
of that calling whatever it may be, and dare to invade

other regions in quest of allies, of understanding friends. But few there are who venture upon these excursions, and even they must return again and again to their own business. Some allies they may have found, but in many eyes they will have looked which give back no gleam of recognition, to many men they will have spoken yet so as not to be understood. And if they ask for an explanation they have to confess that those to whom they made their appeal were warped by the different conditions of their own work.

In every age there have been men who have had in hand and carried in their heart the work and the responsibility of government. How that trust came to be set in them or by what generous arrogance they took upon themselves that task we need not here enquire. Let us assume that the confidence of their fellows was not misplaced, that their own assurance was well grounded in their fitness. It is clear that, if they were to do what they undertook to do, if they were to govern and direct a community, they must devote themselves to that business. If we admit that it is a general, we must also agree that it is a special business, calling for the exercise of no ordinary powers; and that if these powers are to be fully and beneficently exercised they must be cultivated with unremitting care.

The governors of a community must, more than the members of any other class, mind their own business. But, if they mind their own business, how can they know in sufficient detail and with the vivid certainty

of experience any business other than their own?
A general view may be and often is indistinct, and a
general statement colourless. To reflect upon principles may so much tax a man's powers that he has
none to spare for making himself acquainted with
practice in any one of the fields of activity in which
he hopes that his principles will serve for guidance
and support: and men who are engaged day in day
out in these fields may have neither time nor patience
to listen to him. They may even bitterly resent his
counsels, if he offers any; they may bid him mind
his business, meaning that they do not wish him to
mind theirs. Yet it is his business to mind their
business.

Some examples show what is the difficulty in which
a "governor" is placed. A man may hold a pre-
eminent place in politics, he may be acclaimed a
statesman even by his opponents. Let us say that
he comes of a family in which statescraft has been a
long and honourable tradition and in which with the
tradition the equipment of wealth and social distinction have descended as a legacy from generation
to generation; let us say, moreover, that his own
abilities enable him easily and naturally to play,
though no doubt with differences, such as new times
enforce, the part which his people have played before
him. Such a man may, we presume, from time to
time ask himself how much he really knows of the
conditions of life of the multitude over whom he
stands at a height of advantage, perhaps unchallenged
and unquestioned by any critic but himself. Or if he

has critics and if these grudge him his pre-eminence or think him too remote from the daily concerns of his countrymen to be able to judge their needs accurately, must he not at once confess that there is much truth in their censure? What he desires is to understand them; but can he enter into their lives, can he get first-hand knowledge of the lives of merchants and manufacturers and mechanics? Not into the life of any one of them can he enter, and, though he may have reason to suppose that none of them could understand the rest of their fellows in any class better than he does, he knows that he is alone, not merely because he cannot share their daily work, but because he imperfectly understands what to each one of them that work means.

Another man may make his way from an obscure but decent home to a political position where he holds the gaze of his country and of the world; holds it, that is to say, when they have time and inclination to look at him, and indeed many men may look at him with a feeling like family pride as having risen, by merit, "from their ranks." But in his high station he may figure to himself what life was in that particular "rank" from which he came; to that he belonged and not to another; and years of separation from the place of his origin must dim his memory. Sometimes he may long to be restored to his home, but he knows himself to be, for all his affection, not only distanced, but alienated from it. He too dwells alone; he too lacks knowledge of these very conditions with which his early experience might have enabled him, so men think, with special skill and certainty of touch to deal. Again a bishop must mind the business of his diocese or a headmaster of his school; but a bishop or a headmaster may, we conceive, sometimes long to set down the burdens of general administration and take up afresh the vivid work of a parish priest or an assistant master. Yet these men, like others put in authority, are expected to understand men from the routine of whose experience they are necessarily removed. It may be that by a jest of fortune they have been removed from work which they loved for the very reason which might well have bound them to it for ever, namely, that they did it supremely well. The greater their success in their new office, and the better they understand those whom it is their business to direct, the sharper will be their pain in realising that after all they understand but little. If they know where the shoe pinches, they do not know how hard it pinches. They too are isolated and feel the distress of isolation.

Yet once and again a man who has never occupied a place will so speak to men whose lives are spent in it as to make them believe that he understands it better than they, and that he understands them better than they understand themselves. And even he will come short of full comprehension. But we marvel not at his failure, but much rather at his success. How then, we ask, has he done the impossible thing, and won success in conditions which seemed finally to deny it? The pain of solitude he has suffered to refine his spirit as with fire, and meditation has

tempered it, and silence has given it an edge as of
a blade which cuts through the trammels of circum-
stance to the heart of things. Whatever else education
may bring, it must bring willingness to endure pain,
to practise meditation, to keep silence. It will not
of course teach men that they should look for nothing
but pain, take no exercise but meditation, or keep
silence for ever; but it may teach them that in silence
some meanings may be communicated which words
will not carry; that meditation may be had not only
in cloisters but in crowds by those who would bring
their minds to an athletic vigour under its discipline;
that pain is a common possession. It is thus that
loneliness, felt and guessed, becomes a pledge and
bond of society, that individuality becomes significant. These are the gifts which education brings, and
not gifts wholly unlike these—not a bold and cla-
morous speech, not temerity in action, not brazen
advertisement, not the fevered pursuit of pleasure and
advancement. These are not the only gifts of education; but it is by these that any others are to be
tested. We deceive ourselves when we speak of the
gifts of education or its prizes as if they could be
separated from the process of education; and we may
even deceive ourselves by using the plural, for the
gifts of education cannot be sundered one from
another: they are elements in an indivisible whole.

Familiar and necessary figures of speech may mis-
lead us; we must indeed employ them, but with
caution. A runner may win a prize; it is something
which when the race is over he takes away from the

course. But if education is a process its prizes are the sum of the experiences which a man has gained not at the end of the process (for he never attains the end) but at any point at which he may have arrived. So far as we can estimate the sum of his experiences, we know his life, we know what manner of man he is. A man may claim some knowledge of mathematics and music, or of Greek and Latin, or of shorthand and book-keeping, or of plumbing and glazing; if his possessions are only such as can be thus named, then whether they are few or many they will not avail to teach him the general language of men or give him a claim to common humanity; he will speak the language of a class or a coterie or a school and live within its imprisoning conventions and prejudices. With these or without these possessions, and with few or many others of whatever sort, if he has learned the art of silence and of meditation and has endured with his fellows the common pain of solitude, then he can speak the general language and vindicates his part in the commonwealth of men.

If we call a man in whom we recognise this high achievement a good man, are we compelled to say that a man may be equally good whether he is illiterate or learned, skilled or unskilled in any of the crafts and businesses of the world? We may bid a

> Sweet maid, be good,
> And let who will be clever,

because we have to accept cleverness where it exists as a misfortune quite irremediable unless it is cloaked

and happily concealed at last by maid or man whom
years have taught some gentle consideration for other
people. But we shall hardly bring ourselves to say
to boy or girl, to man or woman, "You may be ever
so good, though to be sure you are never so stupid."
There is no need to pretend that goodness cannot
spread its beneficent influence more widely if the
good man commands the instruments of knowledge
and of skill; but he does not command them if they
are merely instruments. To command them he has
to appropriate them as a painter appropriates his
brush, making it one with himself, or a musician his
violin, or a cricketer his bat. Or, if we grant that
these figures of speech ill satisfy us, then we must say
that goodness commands its instruments with a finer
precision, with a more masterful intimacy, than any
other excellence can show.

Will the charge be made that every line in this book
is a plea for a sequestered and impractical mysticism?
The charge is sure to be brought, but not by those
who know by the contrast of sound how to value
silence, by the contrast of quick and varied activities
in the world how to value meditation, by the contrast
of pleasures little or great how to savour the quality
of pain. Sound and activity and pleasures all cease
to be significant for men who will never withdraw
from them; such men have no scale of values and
become incapable of appreciation. It is in silence
that men learn to listen, it is in meditation that
they learn to act, happiness then lightens their
faces when pain has traced upon them its trans-

figuring lines and turned mere suffering into sympathy.

Even this is less than the splendid and surprising truth. The habit of silence, which a man may impose upon himself and commend to his neighbours for their imitation, is itself the habit of listening raised to its highest tension, and yet a habit in which his spirit is so well balanced and so perfectly adjusts its powers that tension is not strain. It gives him the right to enjoy "heard melodies" because he knows that those "unheard are sweeter." Heard melodies may be heard amiss, and variously discussed, each hearer hearing something different from what his neighbours hear. The unheard may be, beyond interpretation, but within acceptance and common understanding, the "music of humanity." It is to this that in silence men attune their ears and so become judges of that fragmentary and incomplete music which forms itself in sounds.

It is men who have practised meditation, and have in that supreme activity made the muscles of their minds at once firm and lissome, who can turn themselves with easy versatility to the distracting engagements of the world, set them in a pattern, give them with order unity, and endure them with an unfaltering courage. Silence and meditation give pain its medicine by making it intelligent. Not that pain is pain the less when it is thus encountered and treated; it is pain the more, and heightened to the pitch where personal becomes universal suffering.

Is this then the end, the object to set before ourselves? So long as education remains a process we may look for nothing better. When the art of conversation has been mastered by all men, then perfection may carry the title of happiness complete and general; but not till then. Till then sensibility will mean a quickness to feel pain, with the vigour and the fortitude to accept and even to welcome it. For, though the barriers which divide men may be weakened and some of them be overthrown, some will still remain. The work of the world includes a variety of labours, done under many conditions. Some of these labours and some of these conditions will tend to make silence rare, and meditation hard, and pain unintelligent. Some silence men may win, and some meditation they may practise wherever their lot may be cast, their loneliness of pain may not be wholly unlit by sympathy and understanding; yet of these good things they will have not enough. The movement of the world seems to be towards more minute and more mechanical specialisation of work and so towards a harder isolation of man from man; and it seems to become more noisy and more rapid as it hurries them breathlessly forward, and so silence and meditation may become for many more difficult to win and to keep. Perhaps we are on the eve of some reorganisation of industry; perhaps scientific discovery is leading us to some fresh unity of law perceived, understood and applied; perhaps philosophy will offer a new and creative re-construction. Yet the dawn is delayed; and till it comes those who have little of the wealth which silence and meditation and sensibility afford must preserve and use what they have; and who knows? perhaps its coming will be hastened by those who, having more than their neighbours of this wealth, may with a "spontaneous and exuberant self-denial[1]" lose it or risk losing it, by taking up the burdens which now weigh most heavily on men who have the least strength to carry them.

[1] Newman, *Parochial and Plain Sermons*, vol. vii, p. 91. Longmans, Green and Co.

For EU product safety concerns, contact us at Calle de José Abascal, 56–1°, 28003 Madrid, Spain or eugpsr@cambridge.org.

www.ingramcontent.com/pod-product-compliance
Ingram Content Group UK Ltd.
Pitfield, Milton Keynes, MK11 3LW, UK
UKHW012328130625
459647UK00009B/140